AWAKENING THE MIND

AWAKENING THE MIND

A GUIDE TO MASTERING
THE POWER OF
YOUR BRAIN WAVES

ANNA WISE

JEREMY P. TARCHER/PUTNAM
a member of Penguin Putnam Inc.
New York

Most Tarcher/Putnam books are available at special quantity discounts for bulk purchase for sales promotions, premiums, fund-raising, and educational needs. Special books or book excerpts also can be created to fit specific needs. For details, write Putnam Special Markets, 375 Hudson Street, New York, NY 10014.

Jeremy P. Tarcher/Putnam
a member of
Penguin Putnam Inc.
375 Hudson Street
New York, NY 10014
www.penguinputnam.com

Library of Congress Cataloging-in-Publication Data

Wise, Anna.
Awakening the mind : a guide to mastering the power
of your brain waves / by Anna Wise.
p.   cm.
ISBN 1-58542-145-6
1. Mental healing.   2. Spiritual healing.   3. Brain.   I. Title.
RZ401 .W77   2002   2001053501
615.8'52—dc21

Printed in the United States of America
1   3   5   7   9   10   8   6   4   2

This book is printed on acid-free paper. ♾

BOOK DESIGN BY MAUNA EICHNER

*This book is dedicated to the many masters
who have given me so much.*

Thank you from the depth of my being.

Acknowledgments

The deep gratitude that I have for those who have supported me in the development of this work and the writing of this book covers a span of decades and people numbering in the thousands. I would like to thank every individual who has helped me on this path of understanding by allowing me to monitor his or her brain waves. My students, clients, trainees, friends, and colleagues from around the world—you have allowed this knowledge to unfold through your own consciousness exploration and desire to awaken your mind and master the power of your brain waves. Thank you for encouraging me and allowing me to do what I love to do.

This work would not have been possible without the amazing wisdom and insight of the late C. Maxwell Cade and the engineering wizardry of Geoffrey Blundell. Thank you also to Isabel Cade and Neil Hancock for the continuing development of the Mind Mirror technology.

My deepest heartfelt gratitude and appreciation go to my dear friend, business partner, and soul sister, Asana Tamaras. Thank you for your tireless dedication, your profound understanding of the work, and your extraordinary personal support. Also my specific acknowledgment and gratitude for your support with this book—

advice, copyediting, hours of listening to me, and your wonderful inside-outside graphics.

I also want to acknowledge and thank a handful of beloved people who have helped me with such commitment—Elizabeth St. John, you are, as always, my sister, healer, friend; Mary Simpkins, you gave me vision, in more ways than one; Steve Miller and Yvonne Schell, your friendship and encouragement just keep on coming; Susan Collet, your assistance has been invaluable; Joshua Leeds, your music sings.

I want to add a special note of appreciation for Sara Carder, my editor—I have so valued your help on this project; and to my publisher Jeremy Tarcher, a true visionary.

The acknowledgments would not be complete without expressing my appreciation and gratitude to my "family" in Taiwan. So many people have touched me from this beautiful island that I cannot even begin to name you all. I am so glad I have found you.

Profound thanks go to Master Wu and your loving family; your healing and commitment have helped me so much. Nancy Lin, thank you deeply for your friendship, support, and help in making Taiwan home. Thanks also to Dr. Olive Liu, Sunny Lo, Sabrina Egan, Dr. Yao, and Agnes Lin from Taipei, and Master Chang from Taisin. A deep and grateful acknowledgment goes to the Matsu Temple in Lukang, to Shu Ling Chang, Mr. Chen Gene Shiang, Dr. Ni Wen Den, and to Tsai-Hong Jen and Mr. Yang from the Quan Yin Temple. Xiexie. Wo hen gan ji nimen. Matsu, thank you. Your boundless compassion and guidance blesses me.

And finally, to my son John; you are truly remarkable, a master-in-the-making, and one of my greatest teachers. With love to infinity, I thank you for traveling with me on this path for so many years. I am blessed to be your mother. Thank you so much for everything.

CONTENTS

AWAKENING
THE MIND

INTRODUCTION

As we settle into the new millennium and move through the changes of the twenty-first century, we bring with us a multitude of technological resources to help with our physical and mental health and well-being. At the same time that science has made unprecedented advances and medical technology has improved beyond recognition, humankind is undergoing an unparalleled evolutionary leap.

A resurgence of spirituality, an increasing awakening of awareness, and a craving for an understanding and experience of the ineffable are now major motivating forces in countless people. If we seriously utilize our latest technological expertise for our spiritual seeking, we can see the wave of the future. This marriage of science and spirituality offers us a new means of mastery, a new mode of self-healing, a new approach to spiritual crisis, a new method of awakening, and a new understanding of mastery.

> The purpose of this book is to teach you first how to meditate and then how to begin to achieve mastery using the marriage of science and spirituality.

For the past twenty-five years, I have been researching and studying the brain-wave patterns of "higher states." This investigation has led me to understand the states of consciousness of the masters and how to replicate and develop this awakening within ourselves. This book will show you how we can now apply our hard-won technological knowledge to the development of mastery. The abilities we learn can be used to enhance and transform our everyday lives.

A Brief History of My Personal Path— How I Got to Here

I began being interested in meditation and higher spiritual states at the age of sixteen, when I had some intangible but decidedly numinous experiences while experimenting with prayer. At the age of eighteen, I almost drowned while tubing in a raging river and went through all of what are now understood to be the classic symptoms of the near-death experience—the light, the tunnel, the music, the bliss, oh the bliss . . .

The problem was that three decades ago I had never heard of these experiences and had no context within which to place my spiritual yearning to return to that bliss without having to die. It took me five years to even verbalize to anyone what had happened. I tried various forms of meditation and attempts at altered states, endeavoring to gain the profound peace that I knew was available inside myself but only fleetingly attainable. I was deterred by the concept of paying high prices for "personal mantras," the need to wear particular colors or clothes, the need to sit in specific positions on particular cushions or wear someone's picture around my neck. So I sought a personal method of meditation.

In 1970, I went to England for summer vacation and ended up staying eleven years. While there, I met Max Cade (C. Maxwell Cade, author of *The Awakened Mind,* 1979). He was a yogi, a scientist, and the father of biofeedback in England, who wanted to see if he could measure the brain waves of higher states of consciousness. To that end, he invented, with the help of engineering wizard Geoffrey Blundell, an EEG he called the Mind Mirror that was specifically designed to measure states of consciousness, as opposed to the medical EEGs of the United States that were designed to identify pathology.

Max took his EEG to swamis and yogis and healers, to people whose states of consciousness we would in some way emulate, to see if there was a commonality among these people. He did indeed find a common brain-wave pattern that kept appearing, regardless of the theology, belief system, technique, or methodology of the individuals. He called this brain-wave pattern **the awakened mind.**

> Every state of consciousness we experience is a combination of one or more of the four categories of brain waves: beta, alpha, theta, and delta. What we will do with this book is learn how to achieve the specific brain-wave patterns of the masters through meditation.

I trained and worked with Max for eight years in London. He taught me to reach the states I was seeking—not in the way that I now teach, but as a Zen master teaches a pupil. I apprenticed with him, assisted him, and became his protégé. Meanwhile, I completed my masters in humanistic psychology at Antioch University's international branch in London, and I co-developed the Natural Dance Workshop with Jim MacRitchie, leading workshops in natural dance in London, Amsterdam, Munich, and other European cities. This gave me many opportunities to integrate meditation with the creative process of dance and performance. I was richly involved in and influenced by the "growth movement" that was happening in Europe at that time, and I was a founding board member of the European Association for Humanistic Psychology based in Geneva.

In 1981, I returned to the United States, with Max's blessings and a Mind Mirror under my arm, to develop the work in my own way. I began expanding the research into areas other than spirituality and healing. I measured artists, composers, dancers, inventors, mathematicians, and scientists. I measured CEOs and presidents of corporations. I found that the brain-wave patterns of high performance, of creativity and the bursts of peak experience, were the same patterns that the yogis and swamis *lived* in. I measured the "ah-ha" or "eureka" experience and found that the brain waves flared into an awakened mind at the exact moment of insight. And it is this brain-wave pattern—the awakened mind—that I teach people to get into.

> Throughout this book you will be learning how to produce the brain-wave pattern of the awakened mind.

I spent from 1981 to 1989 in Boulder, Colorado, developing courses, seminars, and a large private practice, working with the state and content of consciousness and training the awakened mind. I spent more than 6000 hours looking at people's brain waves and understanding how they relate to the individual's state of consciousness. In conducting private sessions, I began with a brain-wave profile to determine a signature pattern. Comparing that to their possible optimum pattern, I helped them to develop their brain waves from where they were at that time to closer to their optimum state. This enabled me to develop a "protocol" for training the awakened mind.

I moved to California in 1989 and now live in Marin County. During the decade of the 1990s, I led seminars worldwide and measured brain waves on five different continents. I also taught and continue to teach frequently at Esalen Institute in Big Sur. In 2000, my long-time assistant and close personal friend, Asana Tamaras, became certified in my work, and together we opened a meditation center in Larkspur, California, where we conduct individual sessions, lead experiential biofeedback meditation workshops, and train others to teach meditation in this way.

Along with the brain-wave *state* training, we also work, perhaps even more closely, with the *content* of consciousness, with how this state can be experienced, applied, and used. From accessing repressed psychological material and suppressed creativity, to using visualization, or what I call "sensualization," for improving health and well-being, to deep spiritual counseling, the work is about teaching people mastery—mastery of the awakened mind brain-wave state and mastery of the content it contains.

> I define mastery as being in the state you want to be in, when you want to be there, knowing what to do with that state, and being able to accomplish it.

When you are in an awakened mind state of mastery, your mind is clearer, sharper, quicker, and more flexible. Emotions are more available, understandable, and easier to transform. Information flows more easily between your conscious, subconscious, and unconscious, increasing intuition, insight, and self-healing abilities. Mastery means being able to enter at will the state of consciousness that is most beneficial and most desirable for any given circumstance, then understanding how to use that state.

THE CONTENTS OF MASTERY

Self-realization and the manifestation of mastery can take many different forms. The most desirable response to any different situation will depend on the contents of that situation and your relationship to it, so there is no way to preordain your optimum response—other than one. That is to say that mastery involves **right action.** Being committed to always having right action means having the integrity that forms the basis or foundation of the contents of mastery. I see mastery as having at least seven different qualities.

QUALITIES OF MASTERY

Compassion

Detachment

Nonjudgment

Clarity

Equanimity

Service

Love

As you develop mastery within yourself, you will expand and personalize your innate understanding of these characteristics, but let's look at a basic definition now, so that you can keep these qualities in mind during your journey through this entire book.

Compassion: understanding and empathy toward your own or another person's difficulty, combined with an attitude or action designed to help.

Detachment: not allowing yourself to be unduly influenced, imbalanced, or negatively affected by the actions of another, and understanding that we cannot force change or perfection on others or ourselves.

Nonjudgment: letting go of criticism and condemnation without losing discernment and insight; eliminating the elements of reproach and blame while maintaining keen perception.

Clarity: having an understanding and certainty that ultimately involves an awareness of a higher spiritual state.

Equanimity: balance, self-possession, self-assurance, and presence of mind that brings calmness, peacefulness, and tranquility.

Service: being aware of and involved in an activity that intrinsically involves some aspect of helping others.

Love: the capacity for tender, warm feeling mixed with joy and deep affection, focused on individuals, humanity in general, and ultimately on a deep, heartfelt devotion to God or divine consciousness.

Please keep these qualities in mind as you develop your *state* of mastery while reading this book. We will begin to address these more in the latter half of the book and specifically in Chapter Nine.

Master Lee Fung Shan, Taiwan's leading Kung Fu master in the Shaolin Monk tradition, says, "The real master emphasizes the importance of following universal principles, qualities, or morals." When I asked him his list of the qualities of mastery, he explained that, as a master who is a "Father-Teacher," his list includes "responsibility, education, leading, nourishing, tolerance, protection, and love." The similarity in these two lists speaks for itself.

THE STATE OF MASTERY

Your brain is producing electrical impulses all of the time. These currents of electricity, or brain waves, are measured in two ways—*amplitude* and *frequency*. The amplitude is the power of the electrical impulse, measured in microvolts. The frequency is the speed of electrical emission measured in cycles per second, or hertz. The frequency determines the *category* of brain wave—*beta, alpha, theta,* or *delta*. The category or combination of categories determines or underlies your state of consciousness at any given time.

Time and time again, I have seen individuals with extraordinary talents, individuals whose states of mind I admire, individuals with higher spiritual awareness, and individuals I consider to be masters hooked up to my EEG to read their brain waves. Like C. Maxwell Cade before me, I have seen that intricate combination of waves that signifies to me that this person truly is *in touch*—with himself, with his innate inner being, with his creativity, with his God.

Expanding on from Max Cade, I have seen that there are many complex and valid varieties of beta, alpha, theta, and delta combinations that represent a state of awakening. I have also noted how it is possible to create some combinations of the four basic categories and *not* be in an awakened-mind state. The prerequisite for an awakened mind is to be able to have an open **flow** of information between the conscious, subconscious, and unconscious mind. The brain creates this possibility in several different ways, which we will be discussing later in the book.

The awakened mind brain-wave pattern doesn't always mean that the individual is *aware* that he or she is awakened, although more often than not they have a deep inner knowledge of their gift. But it means that the *potential* for access to higher states of consciousness and a spiritual awakening is present. All he or she has to do is open up to it and learn how to use it.

To use a twenty-first-century analogy, producing the right brain-wave pattern is like having the right hardware. When you have this particular **state** of mastery, all you have to do is add the right software, use the right **content** in your mind. Using this state of consciousness in the right way will allow you to have greater access to your own inner abilities and powers—to truly have the mind of a master.

What constitutes this state of mastery? You have a multitude of brain waves at any given time. The combination of frequencies your brain is producing determines or underlies the state of consciousness that you are experiencing. Masters have a particular combination of frequencies that allows them to experience the flow of awareness between the conscious, the subconscious, and the unconscious mind. **This combination of frequencies can be learned.**

> The combination of brain-wave frequencies that forms the basis of mastery
> **can be learned**.

When I use an EEG to train this state of consciousness, I look at intricacies like the "interrelationship of the peak frequencies" and the "organization" and "stability" of the brain-wave pattern. But through years of teaching meditation and training brain waves for higher states of consciousness, I have found that certain methods work to access this state of mastery *without using an EEG*. Before we begin the basic training program to develop the brain-wave pattern of the masters, let us look at what these awakened individuals are likely to be experiencing, through understanding their brain waves.

BRAIN WAVES AND CONSCIOUSNESS

Each state that you experience entails a symphony of brain waves, with each frequency playing its own characteristic part. This finely woven, intricate interrelationship of brain-wave frequencies delicately determines your state of consciousness. While you are rarely producing only one type of brain wave at a time, each category of brain waves has its own qualities and characteristics. Let's look first at each of these four categories to gain some insight into the experience and state of mastery.

THE FOUR CATEGORIES OF BRAIN WAVES

BETA

Beta brain waves are the fastest, most common brain-wave pattern for a waking state of consciousness. They are produced by your thinking mind—your conscious thought process. (Hopefully you are producing some right now while reading this book!) Beta is what you use to navigate and negotiate through your everyday life. Your beta can encompass high anxiety and panic—the list-making, judging, critiquing, and continual commenting that can be present in an overactive mind—as well as creative, clear, alert, attentive thinking.

Though beta brain waves are sometimes maligned within consciousness and meditation circles, you need them in order to be able to create and produce in the outside world. In combination with other brain waves, beta is vital to the creative process. Without it, your creativity would stay locked away deep inside, with little chance of being externally expressed.

While beta is a very important component of our state of consciousness, some people tend to live primarily in those faster frequencies alone, without the support of the lower frequencies. Such living can be an anxiety-filled existence, fraught with distracted, unfocused thought processing that makes it difficult for the individual to locate or access the potential of the waves of other categories. At best, beta by itself is a superficial skimming of life.

ALPHA

Alpha brain waves are the next fastest frequencies. Alpha is our relaxed detached awareness, our daydreaming mind. It provides the lucidity and vividness of our imagery. With it we **sensualize,** using all of our senses, not just visual. Alpha is the light reverie that provides the gateway to meditation.

Alpha received much publicity in the late '60s and '70s when it was thought to be the ultimate brain-wave state—the end-all and be-all of brain waves. If you were in your alpha, you were "there." If you could harness it, you were automatically meditating, in a place that was "higher" than normal, and able to accomplish many great things. There is still some hangover of this thinking today, and unfortunately, it just isn't true. While alpha is a vitally important brain wave *in combination with other brain waves,* in and of itself, it is not all that it was thought to be at one time. (You can produce alpha by simply spacing out and watching TV or daydreaming.)

Alpha's primary and indispensable importance is that it is the bridge or link between the conscious and the subconscious mind. It allows you to be aware of what is happening in your deepest dream and meditation states. Without alpha, you won't remember your dreams on waking or be in touch with your deep inner meditation world.

THETA

Theta brain waves are produced by the subconscious mind. They are present in dreaming sleep and the REM (rapid eye movement) state. The subconscious holds our long-term memory and is also the storehouse of creative inspiration and the repository of suppressed creativity, as well as repressed psychological material. Locked away in our theta, and inaccessible unless we have the right combination of other frequencies to access it, can be *anything* we are not in touch with that is somehow buried deep within our psyches—positive or negative. Theta is where we hold our "stuff." If you have any "stuff" (and who doesn't), you know what I'm talking about—the unclear emotional material that each of us collects over the course of our lifetime, sometimes called "baggage" or "garbage."

Paradoxically, theta also provides the experience of deep meditation in a meditation brain-wave pattern. The key to the profundity, bliss, and depth that people look for in meditation is in the theta waves. It is through theta that we make our strongest spiritual connection. In mastery, it is an extremely important brain wave. Theta is the "peak" in the "peak experience." When the other components are in place, it's what allows you to have an "ah-ha" experience. When you want to heal your body or your mind, theta is the place where the healing most readily enters your being and makes a deep, penetrating impact.

DELTA

Delta, the lowest and slowest of all frequencies, is the unconscious mind. Delta is still present when all of the other frequencies turn off in sleep, giving you deep restorative rest. In some people, delta is present in a waking state in combination with other brain waves. As such, it acts as a kind of "radar" or unconscious scanning device that underlies our intuition, our empathy, and our instinctual action. It also offers that true sense of inner knowing that provides deep levels of psychic awareness.

Delta waves are often evident in people in the helping professions—people who need to reach out and enter into someone else's mental, psychological, or emotional being. Delta can also be present in large quantities in hands-on healers and in those who are "people people." However, delta brain waves are not only stimulated by reaching out to understand people. They are also stimulated by reaching out to understand ideas or concepts, objects or artwork, or anything that takes a deep unconscious awareness.

Delta has been called the "orienting response" because it orients us in time and space. Used as our early warning system to sense when danger is present, it's a very primal and animalistic brain wave. Delta waves allow you to glean information that isn't available on a conscious level. From the negative point of view, delta can also be used for hypervigilance. This excessive watchfulness may be a necessary tool for the abused child to use, reaching out with his or her radar to try to ascertain whether Mom is going to come home drunk or Dad is angry enough to hit her. Difficulty develops when this child grows up with the excessive delta continually "reading" the emotional environment and trying to control it for a misguided sense of survival. When this situation can be explained to the mature but hypervigilant adult, the power of the unconscious radar of delta that has been so well developed after all these years can be positively turned around and applied toward extrasensory perception and healing.

Delta has also been connected with the concept of the **collective unconscious.** Whereas theta subconscious insight comes from the very depth of our innermost being and our profound inner spirituality, and is closer to the border of consciousness and more personally meaningful, delta unconscious insight can come from that which is more expansive than the personal or individual. Delta can provide access to a kind of universal psyche or mind. This collective unconscious is a kind of merging of the vast wealth of unconscious understanding and knowledge of humanity that in turn leads to a cosmological or cosmic consciousness. This expanded perception or understanding that taps into the combined unconscious awareness of all sentient life can also initiate a greater knowledge and appreciation of divinity and sense of the Godhead. This is not to say that all people with waking delta experience the collective unconscious, but rather that it is through the gateway of delta that the collective unconscious is most available.

Beta, alpha, theta, and **delta** brain waves are the *building blocks* of your consciousness. They operate in concert—a masterpiece of arrangement, determining and underlying your state of consciousness at any given time.

> Every state of consciousness that we experience is a combination of these four categories of brain waves. The purpose of this book is to help you learn how to achieve the specific brain-wave combination of the masters through meditation and brain-wave training.

THE BRAIN WAVES OF MASTERY

Combining these brain-wave categories intentionally to create a meditation brain-wave pattern is the first stage of mastery. To develop mastery, we start with meditation.

MEDITATION—ALPHA, THETA, AND DELTA

I see meditation as a *state of consciousness*—a specific brain-wave pattern—*not a technique.* There are a multitude of ways to get into that meditation state or brain-wave pattern, from traditional methods of watching your breath, to sitting in silence, to chanting a mantra, to the "modern meditation" techniques of imagery and sensualization, to physical methods such as Yoga, running, or martial arts, to high-performance methods such as the inner arts of tennis, golf, and skiing, to artistic endeavors such as flower arranging, painting, or sculpting. The list is endless.

> Anything that creates the meditation brain-wave pattern within you is the act of meditating—whether you are aware of it or not.

I like to remember the client I had who lived high up in the mountains. She was isolated for long periods of time except for contact with her husband. Somehow, on one of her infrequent trips into town, she found herself in my office. (I never did know who to thank for the referral.) This young woman had a perfect meditation brain-wave pattern. She had never heard of the word "meditation," let alone considered practicing it. She did however "sit in a field of flowers every day." What better meditation could there be?

The opposite extreme of this is the individual who "practiced meditation" for an hour every day for ten years, and felt that she was not really benefiting from it. On measuring her brain waves, I discovered she had been sitting and *thinking* all of that time. She had been practicing a *technique* of meditation, but she had not been meditating. With a few hours of training, she experienced a deep and satisfying alpha, theta, and delta meditation state.

To develop the mind of a master, we need to learn the art of meditation—entering into the state of consciousness and, in particular, the brain-wave pattern of meditation. The presence of both alpha and theta brain waves is important. In this stage, delta is optional, depending on the style of meditation you are doing. If you meditate only in alpha, without the theta waves, you will have a nice relaxing reverie, perhaps vivid colorful imagery and perhaps a sense of detachment and a somewhat expanded awareness, but it will be without the real depth of insight, creativity, spiritual connection, and profundity that is possible from true meditation. If you meditate only in theta without the alpha, you may have a very deep, profound meditation, even bliss, but because theta is *sub*-conscious, you won't remember it! You may even wake up feeling refreshed, alert, and as if you have perhaps learned something—you just won't consciously know what it is. Alpha must be present as the link or bridge in order to draw the information from theta up to the beta thinking mind where it can be processed, interpreted, remembered, and knowingly used.

Delta provides unconscious intuition and insight.

Theta offers deep, subconscious understanding and awareness.

Alpha wraps the lucidity of imagery around the content
so that it can be experienced.

Beta adds conceptual interpretation, explanation, and words.

THE AWAKENED MIND

The brain-wave pattern that we have found in the masters, called the **awakened mind,** is a combination of all four categories—beta, alpha, theta, and delta—in the right relationship and proportion. Since beta is thinking and the combination of alpha, theta, and delta is meditating, you can see that the masters are in a state of thinking and meditating simultaneously, with a flow of connection between the two functions. Someone in the awakened mind brain-wave pattern has access to the unconscious empathy, intuition, and radar of the delta waves; the subconscious creative storehouse, inspiration, and spiritual connection of the theta waves; the bridging capacity, lucidity and vividness of imagery, and relaxed detached awareness of the alpha waves; and the ability to consciously process thoughts in beta—*all at the same time!*

What you don't have in this pattern is the high-frequency beta of the list maker, the judge, the critic—that constant chatter that gets in the way of our optimal functioning. What you do have with an awakened mind is the free flow of information connecting the conscious, subconscious, and unconscious.

In my years of studying brain-wave patterns around the world, I did not necessarily need to know in advance whether the individual I was measuring was a master. For example, one evening in Taipei, I hosted a gathering of professors. Two were friends of mine—Prof. Olive Liu, Ph.D. (who translated my first book into Mandarin), and Prof. Julia J. Tseui, M.D. (who developed a way of proving, by using electromagnetic means, that the meridian energy system exists). Prof. Tseui brought a friend of hers I had not met before, Prof. Kuo-Gen Chen, to see me. She told me only that he was a professor of physics at Soochow University of Taipei and was very interested in my biofeedback equipment. As a favor, I hooked him up to the Mind Mirror.

Frankly, I had expected a rather dry evening of academia. When I saw his absolutely perfect brain-wave state after less than a minute of meditation, I pointed to the machine in astonishment. My friend said, "Oh, I forgot to tell you he is a Chi Kung master."

One of the masters that Max Cade did his original research with in identifying the awakened mind brain-wave pattern was a spiritual teacher named Swami Prakashanand. Max asked the swami the question, "How many times a day do you meditate?" This was the mid-1970s, and at that time, I hoped I would hear the true secret of meditation—the formula. For example: get up at 4 A.M. and meditate for an hour; eat, meditate again; etc., etc. His answer to the question

How many times a day do you meditate? was very simple. "Once a day, for twenty-four hours," he said.

That is what living in an awakened mind is like. The state of meditation is constant, and you can turn thoughts off and on at will. The content or the material of the mind may change, but the state is one of awakening regardless. In this book, I will not try to teach you how to live in that state constantly, but how to access it, develop it, and eventually enter it at will. With that skill, the amount of time you spend in it will become potentially greater and will be a matter of personal choice.

The quickest and easiest way to begin to learn how to develop an awakened mind is through meditation. Once you have developed the alpha, theta, and delta of the meditation brain-wave pattern without beta (i.e., without thought), then you can add the beta back in the appropriate way to create an awakened mind. While having the mind of a master *is* a combination of meditation and thinking at the same time, it *is not* just random thought added to meditation. For conscious awakening, we will add the beta back to meditation in very specific ways. But we must first learn to get rid of it.

This book describes a step-by-step process. Each chapter provides instruction, exercises, and meditations that will guide you in developing an awakened mind. First, we will look at the basic foundations of mastery. In Chapter One, relaxing the body and stilling the mind set the stage and prepare you for the brain-wave and consciousness training to come. In Chapter Two, alpha development creates the bridge to the subconscious mind and provides lucidity, clarity, and vividness within. In Chapters Three and Four, accessing and experiencing the deep inner self found in the most subconscious and unconscious brain waves of theta and delta hold the key to the depth and profundity of creativity, insight, intuition, healing, and all expressions of mastery. And, finally, adding external awareness and conscious thought to this inner meditation state allows you to put the pieces together and experience the awakened mind state of mastery as explained in Chapter Five.

The next few chapters after those will address some of the more personally transformative and spiritual aspects of mastery. Chapter Six will teach you more about the processes of using meditation for self-exploration and different ways of identifying and exploring inner blocks. Chapter Seven teaches methods for healing the blocks. Chapter Eight introduces the relationship of the energy system and kundalini to brain waves and mastery. Chapter Nine addresses the personal qualities of mastery and also covers challenges that might occur to you while awakening your mind, and Chapter Ten looks at the bigger picture of meditation and awakening.

A Few Pointers for Your Meditation Practice

HOW OFTEN SHOULD I PRACTICE?

The amount and frequency for which you practice meditation is very personal and individual. Please do not set goals that are beyond what is actually possible or reasonable for you. That is a recipe for failure, and meditation can quickly become a thing of your past rather than of your present. If at any time you feel like you are failing, then your goals are too high.

Instead, allow yourself to build up the amount that you meditate in a comfortable and progressive way. I would rather you meditate as little as five minutes twice a week feeling successful about it and gaining the benefit from it than set yourself a goal of half an hour or an hour a day and then not do it. There are a number of "one-minute meditations" in Chapter One that are useful practices in and of themselves. Just one minute of successful inner contemplation, relaxation, and meditation can be a very big step on the road to eventual mastery.

Optimally, begin by trying fifteen to thirty minutes two or three times a week. See how that feels. If that is hard to accomplish, reduce the amount. You might prefer meditating for only one to five minutes two or three times a week. Mix and match according to your need. If it is easy and you find yourself craving more, increase it. Remember, the awakened mind can come in an instant of "ah-ha," but the seed of mastery that you plant inside yourself also needs time to germinate and flower.

SHOULD I LISTEN TO MUSIC WHILE I MEDITATE?

In my workshops and individual sessions, I use music in addition to my voice to help take people down into themselves. We have found that the more internalized and more still they get, the quieter the music can be. In fact, I often use the volume of the music as an aid to take people into meditation more quickly. As I reduce the volume of the music, the meditator gets quieter and quieter inside in order to be able to hear it.

Use gentle, noninvasive, nonmelodic music as a pad to lean on in the silence of your inner meditation. Stay away from tunes that are familiar that you might want to hum along with. Actually, stay away from tunes as a whole. If you find yourself listening to the music then you are doing just that—listening to music, not meditating. So therefore, I advise that you choose soft, quiet, gentle, non-melodic background sounds that can peacefully fill the external void as you enter and expand deep within yourself.

WHAT POSITION SHOULD I MEDITATE IN?

You have a choice of sitting or lying flat while meditating. Try both to see how you respond. In either case, your spine should be straight and in alignment so that the energy can flow properly.

Meditating lying down generally allows the beta to still more easily, but also involves the danger of falling asleep. People have a greater tendency to lose their alpha and go directly to a deep theta or even delta state in the lying-down position. If this happens to you, definitely try sitting up. Occasionally, even while sitting up, people may "disappear." In that case, I have asked the meditator to hold a glass of water while meditating and have had frequent success.

MEDITATE WITH YOUR EYES CLOSED

Begin by meditating with your eyes closed, as alpha is produced *much more easily* during closed-eye meditation. Opening the eyes tends to immediately turn off the alpha in many people. Later, you can begin to open your eyes gently if you wish.

ENJOY!

There is a wealth of information here for you to work with and enjoy. Allow yourself to repeat each practice as many times as you wish and continue delving deeper and deeper into yourself—into awakening your mind and mastering the power of your brain waves.

THE FOUNDATIONS
OF MASTERY

Relaxing the Body and
Stilling the Mind

Underlying mastery is the ability to control both the body and the mind to create the state and the content of consciousness that is desired or appropriate at any given time. It is much easier to learn to master your brain-wave state from the perspective of a relaxed body than from a place of stress and tension. Try gritting your teeth, making a fist, tightening your muscles, and through clenched jaws uttering, "I WILL be creative." This approach is stressful at best and rarely works to elicit optimum functioning and high performance, not to mention a sense of spirituality and mastery.

Mastery is best accomplished by *allowing* the state to occur with a relaxed body and an open and quiet mind. In turn, the accomplishment of mastery itself engenders a relaxed body and a peaceful mind. Learning to *intentionally and consciously* relax the body and still the mind begins the process of self control of internal states that can lead you to greater control of the more refined and complex brain-wave patterns that give rise to higher states of consciousness.

> Relaxation clears the path and opens the door to an easier journey into meditation and the deeper self.

RELAXING THE BODY

To begin with, you can approach relaxation as a complete practice within itself. In later stages of your training, you will probably find that you still want to practice a few minutes of physical relaxation before you dive into the depths of your meditation. It always clears the path and opens the door to an easier journey into the deeper self.

There are several ways of practicing this relaxation and the other meditations and exercises that you find in this book. The first is to read through the exercise or meditation from beginning to end. Make a mental note of the general idea of what you hope to accomplish during the meditation. Don't try to remember this goal word for word, but rather get a *feel* for it. If you imbed the instructions deep inside, you won't have to activate your beta waves to tell yourself what to do. You may want to pick out key images or stepping-stones to help you remember the order of the instructions. Then close the book, close your eyes, and take the appropriate position—either sitting or lying down. Allow yourself to re-create inside what you have just read. Try not to talk to yourself or use words to instruct yourself—just allow it to happen.

You may wish to read the meditation into a cassette recorder and then play it back to yourself. Having instructions to follow may allow you to turn off your thoughts more easily and *surrender* to the relaxation. Also, a voice gently droning in the background gives you something to lean against that often lets you go deeper inside yourself. Be sure to speak slowly and clearly, with a relaxed tone. Allow yourself many long pauses with no instructions, so that you can have plenty of time to feel the experience inside. Initially, you may be a bit surprised by the sound of your own voice. This should pass after you have listened to the recording a few times.

Another alternative is to have a friend read the meditation to you. Be sure he or she follows the same instructions to speak with a relaxed voice and allow you ample quiet time. When reading these meditations into a tape recorder or giving them to another person, you may find the need to speak more slowly than you would anticipate. You may even wish to start a small group meeting, taking turns with one person reading while the rest are meditating.

I have also made CDs and cassette tapes of some of these meditations. To order these, see the contact information on page 256.

You may practice the following relaxation either sitting or lying down. If you sit, you may wish to lean back against the back of the chair or against the wall if you are sitting on the floor. For this practice, sit unsupported only if you find that you tend to fall asleep during the relaxation. The slight discomfort and need for muscular tension that is caused by the upright sitting will probably be enough to keep you awake. When practicing deep psycho-physiological relaxation with my clients, I usually have them use a recliner for maximum comfort, depth, and ability to let go.

You may also practice lying down—however, a brief note of warning: If you are not used to lying-down meditations, the very act of lying down can signal a sleep response—especially if you are lying in or on your bed. If you want to practice horizontally, I would suggest that you lie on the floor, perhaps with cushions under your head and knees to prevent strain on your back. The unfamiliarity of this alone may be enough to prevent sleep. Combine that with the hardness of the floor (carpet or mat suggested!) and you should be able to remain conscious throughout.

Make sure the room is the right temperature. If necessary, fault on the side of warmth. Lying in a room that is too cold is not conducive to relaxation and may even increase your tension as your body fights the cold. Don't just hike up the heat, since too much warmth might also give you a tendency to fall asleep. A light blanket will keep your body warm during relaxation.

Deep Relaxation

The next space of time is a time for yourself,
A journey inside to calm, soothe, heal, and relax
Your body, mind, and spirit.

Begin by closing your eyes.
Allow your mind to clear of all thoughts,
and focus on your breathing.

Breathing easily and deeply . . .
easily and deeply . . .
Breathing relaxation into your body,
and breathing away any tension.
Breathing relaxation into your mind,
and breathing away any thoughts.

Very gently begin to withdraw yourself from the outside
    environment . . .
Withdraw yourself from your surroundings . . .
Withdraw yourself from any remaining thoughts . . .
Withdraw yourself into yourself . . .
Into your own silence . . .
Into your own serenity . . .
Into your own peace.
And relax.

■ ■ ■

(indicates a pause)

Allow the muscles of your face to relax . . .
Your forehead, the muscles around your eyes, the muscles behind
your eyes . . .
Your lips, tongue, throat, and jaws . . .
. . . all deeply relaxed.

Allow the relaxation to flow down through your neck . . .
into your shoulders.
Allow it to flow down both arms . . .
all the way to your fingertips.
Allow the relaxation to flow into your chest . . .
And down your back and spine . . .
. . . allowing the muscles of your back to just let go.
You let go . . .
you let go . . .
you just . . .
let . . .
go . . .

■ ■ ■

Take the relaxation down through your torso
And allow it to go deep into your stomach . . .
Right into the very center of your body . . .
Right into the very center of your being . . .

Allow the relaxation to flow down through your hips and pelvis . . .
Allow the relaxation to flow down both legs . . .
. . . all the way to your feet . . .
and toes.

So that deep within yourself, you can visualize and experience your
  whole body as completely relaxed . . .
Deep within yourself, you can visualize and experience your mind
  as quiet and still . . .
. . . very still.
Deep within yourself, you can visualize and experience your
  emotions as calm and clear . . .
. . . your spirit as peaceful.
Deep within yourself, you can visualize and experience
your body, mind, emotions, and spirit
in harmony.

■ ■ ■

Stillness . . . Silence . . . Rest . . . Peace . . .

Very gradually begin to allow yourself to find an image, symbol,
  word, or phrase that describes how you are feeling right now.

And now . . .
In your own time . . .
When you are ready . . .
Very gently begin to allow yourself to find a closure for your
  meditation . . .
Taking all of the time that you need to come to completion inside,
allow yourself to reawaken and return . . .
. . . back to the outside space . . . feeling alert and refreshed.

Take several deep breaths, and allow yourself to stretch . . .
beginning with your fingers and toes.
Take a full body stretch,
and allow yourself to return to an upright sitting position.

Allow yourself to reflect:

- *Before you resume your normal activity, take a few moments to reflect on your experience.*

- *Remember your image, symbol, words, or phrase at the end.*

- *Remember what it felt like to be so deeply relaxed, and once again relate that feeling to the representative symbol or words you chose.*

The next time you want to relax, recall this cue. By remembering the images or words, you can recall the memory of relaxation in your body and mind and reenter the state of relaxation much more easily and quickly.

AFTER THE MEDITATION . . .

How you complete your meditation can have a major impact on what you gain from the experience and your ongoing development of mastery. Don't just suddenly say, "Oh, I've got to stop!" and jump up out of the meditation. This is a recipe for losing the memory of the meditation, as well as being an uncomfortable way to conclude.

> Crystallize your experience into a few images, symbols, colors, sensations, or words.

First, before you leave the meditation state, crystallize your experience into a few images, symbols, colors, sensations, or words. As you reawaken, bring these into your beta mind by writing them down, speaking them, or at least thinking about them. Reactivate your body slowly. You want your reemergence to be pleasurable and complete. Start with the periphery—moving, stretching, and wiggling your fingers and toes—and let that turn slowly into a full-body stretch. Take several deep and somewhat rapid breaths.

Notice what it feels like as you reawaken. This will give you important biological feedback that will show you the difference between the meditation state and the waking state. **The more you can become aware of the difference in these two states and the sensations of the journey between them, the more you can learn to master that journey.**

The sensory experiences, images, colors, feelings, and words that you bring back with you from your relaxation can be used as what I call **keys** or **landmarks.** They act as signposts on the journey into yourself, both to tell you where you are and to help you map and navigate your inner landscape more easily, quickly, and effectively. You can ground your relaxation by bringing the experience that you had in your lower frequencies of alpha, theta, and delta up to your conscious mind of beta. This usually means putting it into words so that you can remember it and communicate about it. The more you do this, the more you open up the channels of information that flow between the subconscious and conscious mind, facilitating the awakened mind brain-wave pattern.

There are two kinds of landmarks, those that relate to content and those that relate to state. Those that relate to content are very personal and unique to each individual. You may experience your relaxation as being set in a serene, fragrant, and colorful garden area, whereas your friend following the exact same relaxation may be more focused on a blue light that seems to surround him and have no other environmental awareness. Both landmarks are equally valid as keys to helping you return to your own individual best depth of relaxation. If you write, speak, or even just think about these landmarks after a meditation, you will remember them more easily and be able more readily to return to the state of consciousness that they engender by simply envisioning them or re-creating them the next time you want to relax or meditate.

There are other forms of subjective landmarks that are more universal in nature. While still subjective, these are sensations and experiences often commonly shared by people as they alter their brain-wave states and begin to develop mastery. Reviewing the Table of Subjective Landmarks (on page 30) after every meditation that involves deep relaxation will help you begin to identify the keys to your higher states much more readily. Each of these landmarks is related to a possible brain-wave (EEG) pattern that you are likely to be producing at the time you experience it. This chart can act as a kind of **biofeedback** that you can use as a guide to help you know when you are returning to that state and actually help you return to it more quickly and easily.

Let's take a look at these seven categories. Just about everyone spends a little bit of time in Category Zero at the beginning of his or her meditation. How quickly you can pass through this stage depends on how easily you can relax your body and still your mind.

In Category One, you may still feel distracted and a little bit scattered, but it is not your normal everyday externalized thinking state. It is possible to have the feeling of being "stuck" in this state by simply continuing to feel that, instead of meditating, you are about to go to sleep and you are desperately trying to prevent that. Should this happen to you, it is best to arouse yourself again, take several deep breaths to really awaken (almost to the point of hyperventilation but not quite—only enough to really wake yourself up), and then start your meditation again. I have even asked students who were stuck in this state to get up and run around the backyard to arouse their body and mind properly so that they could begin meditation in an appropriate body/mind state.

Category Two can truly be a sense of being in between states— not clearly awake and yet not really meditating. If you feel like you are stuck in this state, the trick is to just relax a little bit more and let yourself go deeper. Try doing it on the exhalation. When you breathe out, allow yourself to experience a release of tension that lets you go down underneath this transitional state.

TABLE OF SUBJECTIVE LANDMARKS

Cat.	Subjective Landmarks	EEG
0	• Just beginning to relax • A feeling of "settling down" • Some difficulty in stilling the mind • Itchy state • A feeling of "Why am I doing this?"	Continuous beta, often with some flares of other waves. Possibly intermittent alpha.
1	• Befogged consciousness • Feeling dizzy • Sensations of going under an anesthetic • Occasional feeling of nausea • Mind filled with everyday affairs—almost as an avoidance of inner stillness • A feeling of scattered energies • A sensation of drifting off to sleep or being pulled back from the edge of sleep	Somewhat reduced beta, but still present. Intermittent but stronger alpha.
2	• Energies beginning to collect • Beginning to feel calmness and relaxation • Uninvited vivid flashes of imagery • Childhood flashbacks • Images from the distant to the immediate past • Attention not very sustained • A feeling of being "in between states"	Reduced beta. Stronger alpha, could be continuous. Intermittent (low-frequency) theta.
3	• Well-defined state • Pleasant bodily sensations of floating, lightness, rocking, or swaying • Occasional slight rhythmical movement • More sustained concentration • Increased and clearer imagery • Increased ability to follow guided imagery	Highly reduced beta. Continuous alpha. Possibly more continuous theta with increased frequency and/or amplitude.

Cat.	Subjective Landmarks	EEG
4	• Extremely vivid awareness of breathing • Extremely vivid awareness of heartbeat, blood flow, or other bodily sensations • Feeling of loss of body boundaries • Sensation of numbness in limbs • Sensation of being full of air • Sensation of growing to great size or becoming very small • Sensation of great heaviness or lightness • Sometimes an alternation between internal and external awareness	Highly reduced beta. Continuous alpha. Increased theta.
5	• Very lucid state of consciousness • Feeling of deep satisfaction • Intense alertness, calmness, and detachment • Sensation of "spacing out" or disappearing from the environment and/or body • Extremely vivid imagery when desired • Feeling of altered state lacking in previous categories 0 to 4	Possible deep meditation or awakened mind with varying combinations of beta mastery and continuous alpha and theta, with or without delta.
6	• New way of feeling • Intuitive insight into old problems, as though seen from a more aware level • Synthesis of opposites into a higher unity • Sensation of being surrounded in light • A feeling of higher spiritual awareness • A sensation that "nothing matters" other than just being • A feeling of greater knowledge of the universe	Four possible patterns: 1. Awakened Mind (beta, alpha, theta, delta) 2. Optimum meditation (alpha, theta, delta) 3. Very little electrical brain-wave activity 4. Evolved mind (beta, alpha, theta, and delta with no blocks)

Category Three is really the beginning of meditation. It gives you light, gentle, pleasant sensations of relaxation, sometimes involving slight, gentle, or almost imperceptible rocking and swaying motions. You could stay in this state and have a valid, enjoyable, and meaningful relaxation and meditation. However, Category Three does not represent the deepest, most profound states of meditation or the experience of mastery. So if you can, you want to let go and move deeper.

Many people are not aware that the experience of Category Four is actually deeper than Category Three. Some people find this an uncomfortable state. It is very physical in the majority of cases, with potentially odd body sensations. Often in meditation, when people reach this state, they mistakenly feel that they have stopped meditating, and they "back away from it" back up into Category Three—out of either fear or a misinterpretation that they have somehow aroused up out of meditation. Because of this, they may never allow themselves to move deeper than Category Three, fearing the sensations that occur in Four. Instead, try to let yourself welcome the experiences in Category Four if they occur. See them as landmarks that tell you how deep you are, and simply allow yourself to relax even deeper, down through the sensations into Category Five.

Category Five can be a deeply profound meditation, or even a strong awakened mind or "ah-ha" experience. It may come initially only in a brief flash of a split second. Many people have the tendency to discount this experience, saying, "That didn't really happen" or, "That wasn't the real thing because it wasn't long enough." This is an unfortunate attitude to take as it gives the subconscious mind the message that the split second of awakening that you experienced did not really happen or is irrelevant. This internal discounting may even signal the subconscious mind not to return to that state, as it wasn't really real.

On the other hand, if you can acknowledge that split second of clarity and satisfaction, you can plant a landmark there and make it much easier to return. The next time, you may have two split seconds of awakening or even a whole second. The following time, you may have two seconds . . . and so on. Category Five is a very pleasing, lucid, and clear state. After some practice, it may be possible to spend a large portion of your meditation having this experience. This is truly practicing your state of mastery.

We're not trying to train Category Six in this book; however, you may enter this bliss state during your meditation. If so, allow yourself to acknowledge it, no matter how brief it is, and enjoy the experience.

When we're meditating, it would be nice to think that we start at Category Zero and quickly and easily drop down through each successive category to the place where we stop to meditate— Three, Four, Five, or Six. Unfortunately, this is just not the way that it works. It is possible for us to move around on this scale rapidly and seemingly randomly as our mind settles. For example, you may experience Category Zero, then Two, Four, One, Three, Five, then "Oh my gosh, I'm meditating!" and back up to Zero.

> Mastery comes from learning how to be where you want to be on this scale, when you want to be there.

STILLING THE MIND

The second foundation of mastery is learning to quiet the mind. "Still the squirming of the worm in the brain," said Patanjali, second-century B.C. author of the Yoga-Sutra. Mind chatter is a universal problem. Do you ever experience an inner voice constantly talking to you, perhaps in the form of a judge or critic, or perhaps just as a commentator or narrator describing what is happening? Maybe you have a list maker inside or carry on imaginary dialogues with your boss, friend, colleague, or spouse. Is it ever in the form of the great "should"—"you should this" and "you should that"? True mastery requires calming your mind and stilling this voice.

Other voices or thoughts need stilling, too. To eliminate beta brain waves and experience the space of meditation where no thought occurs, you also must, for the time being, put aside your work and family concerns, your creative thoughts, your plans, ideas, and goals that occupy your thinking, conscious mind. You will be able to return to them later with greater clarity, insight, and manifestation power (the ability to materialize your creative inspiration).

Try this experiment to help you better understand how your thoughts operate.

BECOMING AWARE OF THOUGHTS

Stop and sit for one minute.
 Keeping your eyes open, do not try to alter your thoughts or
  control your mind in any way.
You can, if you wish, time yourself on a watch or clock.

Allow yourself to reflect:

- *What happened to your mind during that one minute?*

- *How many thoughts did you have?*

- *Where did they come from?*

- *What was the content or subject matter of your mind during that minute?*

- *How many times did you change the subject?*

- *Were you completely aware of your thoughts as they were happening; or was there a running commentary somewhere in the back of your mind that you could tune into or tune out of?*

- *Can you imagine what the experience would have been like to spend that minute with a still mind?*

One of the most important things you can do to help quiet your mind when relaxing and beginning to meditate is very simple and takes no time at all. You will be surprised, even amazed, at the effect that this easy yet essential practice has on your internal state of consciousness.

Stop for a minute to try this practice:

Relaxing Your Tongue

Close your eyes and allow your tongue to relax.
No one will be looking at you, so it's OK to let your mouth hang
    open slightly.

Just simply let your tongue go, especially the back of your tongue.
As you exhale, you can feel it let go even more.
Exaggerate the relaxation.
Exaggerate it again.

You can almost feel your tongue floating in the cavity of your
    mouth.
You may feel it shorten some—or thicken.

Exaggerate the relaxation even more.
Focus only on relaxing your tongue—nothing else.

And now think . . .

Think hard.

Think.

Think!!!

Allow yourself to reflect:

- *What happened?*
- *Did you have any difficulty thinking?*
- *Did your tongue tense up?*

There are really only two reactions to that exercise. Either you will have had some difficulty in thinking, or just not really *want* to think, or your tongue will begin to tighten in preparation for **subvocalization.**

> We think with our tongues!

. . . metaphorically speaking, anyway. When people think, they have a tendency to talk to themselves. Even if you are not aware of this subvocalization, your tongue will feel tense—ready for action—when you are thinking. You may experience this as a gentle pulling on the back of your tongue, or you may not feel it at all. If you relax your tongue *completely,* you cannot talk to yourself. Therefore, it is much more difficult to think. It is a simple technique that will help you radically reduce your beta brain waves and begin to still your mind immediately. **If you take nothing else away with you from reading this book, you will have gained enormously from this one practice.** (My students say that you may be able to cut ten years off of sitting in the cave waiting for your thoughts to clear!)

IF IN DOUBT, LIE DOWN

Another factor besides tongue relaxation that can greatly affect your beta production is the position in which you are meditating. I have found that students who have difficulty with reducing their "splayed beta" (high-amplitude, high-frequency beta indicating anxiety or inability to stop thinking) while they are sitting in meditation do much better lying down. The very act of lying down seems to begin to reduce the beta by itself. Then as the meditation continues, the mind becomes stiller and quieter much more easily.

SLOW YOUR BREATHING DOWN

A third factor that can influence the reduction of thoughts is to slow your breathing down. The calmer and deeper you can make your breathing—without creating effort or strain, or holding your breath—the more quickly and easily you can still your mind. I do not advocate breathing at any particular rate, which is why, when I teach, I do not have people breathe *with* me at the rate I am breathing. People breathe at different rates according to their lung capacities and other personal factors. However, if you can slow your own breathing down in relation to your own norm, you will not only relax more deeply, you will enter a state of meditation more quickly.

Try another experiment. Let's find your norm.

COUNTING YOUR BREATH

Time yourself for one minute, and count how many breaths you have during that time.

Do not try to alter your "normal" breathing rate.
One complete breath cycle of inhalation and exhalation is one
count.

The average number of breaths per minute is between twelve
and eighteen. What is *your* normal number of breaths per minute?
If you focus on your breathing and allow it to slow down, you will
instantly reduce your beta brain-wave activity.

Try this exercise sitting with your eyes closed if you have a timer.
Otherwise, practice while looking at your watch.

SLOWING YOUR BREATHING

Lightly place your hand palm-down on your thigh.
As you inhale, slowly raise your hand.
As you exhale, slowly lower it again.
In this way, simply use your hand as a lever to gently begin to
regulate your breathing and slow it down.

It is important to make sure you are not forcing yourself to slow
your breathing.
Nor should you hold your breath or in any way starve yourself of
oxygen.
You simply have an *intention* of slowing your breath.
You may wish also to linger a little longer than usual at the points of
full inhalation and full exhalation.
However, there should be absolutely no strain.

Once again, time yourself, and allow yourself to count the
number of breaths that you have in one minute,
this time intentionally slowing your breathing rate in the manner
described above.

Allow yourself to reflect:

- *How many breaths did you take this time?*
- *Was it fewer than before?*
- *How long did the minute seem? Longer or shorter than the first minute you timed?*
- *What were your thoughts like compared to the minute you timed earlier?*
- *Did you remember to keep your tongue relaxed?*
- *How do you feel?*

Notice what only one minute of slowing your breath can do to your sense of stress or relaxation.

With these three simple instructions, *relax your tongue, recline or lie down,* and *slow your breathing by counting your breaths,* you can dramatically alter your state of consciousness in just one minute.

There are a number of other techniques for stilling the mind that you may also wish to experiment with.

Withdrawal into yourself in meditation is another excellent means of leaving unwanted thoughts behind. Get into a comfortable position, allow your eyes to close, and take a few moments to relax again.

WITHDRAWAL FROM YOUR THOUGHTS

Send your awareness outside of the building you are in—into the street.

Become aware of external noises.

You may also be aware of the energy and atmosphere outside the building, especially if there is traffic or there are people moving around.

Try not to label the noises or energetic vibrations, but just be aware of any sounds that you may hear.

Gently withdraw yourself from the outside environment into the
building.
Try to take in the whole building, no matter how large it is.
Become aware of any sounds, energies, or movements within the
building.

Now gently withdraw yourself from the rest of the building into the
room that you are in. Become aware of the sounds, energies, and
atmosphere of the room that you are in.

Now gently withdraw yourself from the room into your own body—
into yourself.
Become aware of the sounds, sensations, movements, and energies
within your own body.

Now finally withdraw yourself from your body into a place inside
yourself where there is stillness—into your center.

There exists inside you a place of stillness, silence, and peace.
Find the place inside that is quiet, and allow yourself to rest in that
place for a minute or two.

Anytime a thought comes through, relax your tongue and return to
that place of stillness.

■ ■ ■

As you prepare to return to the outside space,
very gradually begin to be aware of what you are experiencing—
the feeling of relaxation in your body, the contents of your mind,
and once again be aware of the place of peace and stillness inside.

You may wish to find a few keys for what this feels like,
to help you return to this state of consciousness more easily and
effortlessly.

These keys or landmarks might be a body sensation, a color, a word, an image, or even a sound.

After doing these exercises, take several deep breaths and allow yourself to stretch and reawaken fully, feeling alert and refreshed. Make sure that you are completely back in the outside environment before you begin dealing with it.

These exercises can take you deeper into yourself than you are consciously aware of. Don't drive a car or operate any dangerous equipment without making sure you are fully back.

Withdrawal like this can be useful in another way as well. If, while you are relaxing or meditating, there is a loud sound or disturbance outside (and if it's obviously something you don't need to attend to), *use the disturbance as an aid to take you deeper into yourself by consciously withdrawing from it.* Every time you hear the disturbance, it becomes an almost welcome signal or reminder to withdraw. This is a useful way to reframe a noise over which you have no control.

CONCENTRATION EXERCISES

OUTER FOCUS

Learning to focus your attention without letting your mind wander will greatly reduce beta waves. It will also expand your awareness and make achieving a meditative state easier.

Begin the following exercise sitting with your eyes open. Choose a spot a few feet in front of you at slightly lower than eye level to look at. You may place something in front of you or use an already existing ordinary object in your room. People often choose a flower, a design such as a mandala, or an icon of some sort for the aesthetic value, but the object of the exercise is to gaze at an unidentifiable spot, so if you choose something like a flower, identify one spot on the flower to look at—not the whole flower. I know some people who are completely satisfied gazing at a spot on the carpet.

You can use your timer for this exercise if you wish, or simply practice it for about a minute. Sometimes you may be surprised as your "minute" stretches into a longer time period.

External Spot

Sitting comfortably with your back straight,
send your awareness outward to the spot you have chosen.
Become aware only of the spot.
Let your awareness move outward in a straight line, like an arrow,
from you to the spot.
Let your eyes relax,
and unfocus your vision.
The spot may become hazy or clouded.
(Remember, you are not focusing on an identifiable object—only on
    a location.)
Allow your mind to clear of all thoughts and images
as you focus only on your spot
without thought
for one minute.

Allow yourself to reflect:

- *How many thoughts did you have?*

- *How long did the minute seem?*

- *Were you able to maintain your focus?*

Sometimes people have difficulty maintaining focus on one external spot and would prefer to have a kind of expanded or diffuse awareness instead. Try this next.

DIFFUSE EXTERNAL AWARENESS

Sit comfortably, with your eyes open.
Send your awareness outward
and let it expand to cover the broadest possible perimeters.

Let your eyes become soft and very unfocused,
and experience a kind of diffuse awareness of your entire range of
    vision at once,
without focusing on any particular area or spot.

Allow your mind to clear of all thoughts,
as you sit,
concentrating on your external expanded awareness.

Diffuse awareness of your whole environment,
without thought
for one minute.

Allow yourself to reflect:

- *How many times did your mind wander?*

- *Was it easier or harder than focusing on a fixed spot?*

INNER FOCUS

Some people prefer to focus on something within instead of something outside. If you feel more comfortable with this technique, choose a spot *inside* on which to concentrate. Favorite areas among the people I have worked with include the heart area, the navel, between the eyebrows, the center of the forehead, and the crown of the head. Your spot, however, could be anywhere inside that is comfortable—even your left big toe. Practice this exercise with your eyes closed.

INTERNAL SPOT

Close your eyes and sit comfortably,
sending your awareness inside,
and, like an arrow pointed inward, focus on the spot you have
    chosen.
Allow your mind to clear of all thoughts,
as you concentrate only inside,
on your spot,
without thought
for one minute.

Allow yourself to reflect:

- *How many thoughts did you have?*

- *Did you maintain the same spot or did it change or move?*

- *Was this easier or harder than focusing on the external spot?*

- *Did the time seem longer or shorter?*

Sometimes, people have difficulty maintaining focus on one inner spot and would prefer to concentrate on their whole body from the inside. Try this next.

DIFFUSE INTERNAL AWARENESS

Sit comfortably, with your eyes closed.
Send your awareness inward

and let it be diffuse throughout your whole body.
You may experience it as being aware of your body from the
   inside . . .

Almost like being inside the empty shell of your body,
Allow your mind to clear of all thoughts,
as you sit,
concentrating on your *whole body* from the inside.
Diffuse awareness of your whole body
from the inside
without thought
for one minute.

Allow yourself to reflect:

   • *How many times did your mind wander?*

   • *Was it easier or harder than focusing on a fixed spot inside?*

For the final concentration exercise, choose which form of inner
concentration you prefer—diffuse or spot.

INTERNAL AND EXTERNAL

Begin by sitting comfortably with your eyes closed.
Focus inside, either on your inner spot or diffuse throughout your
   body.
With your mind clear, send your awareness only inward.

When you feel you have achieved your inner focus,
maintain it, and at the same time slowly open your eyes
(just a few eyelashes will do at first)
and send your awareness outward to either focus on your spot

or have expanded diffuse external awareness
so that you are aware both inside and outside
at the same time.

You are focusing on yourself from the inside with awareness moving
  inward
and focusing on the outside with awareness moving outward at the
  same time,
keeping your eyes open
without thought
for one minute.

Allow yourself to reflect:

- *Was it easier or harder than the other exercises?*

- *How long did the minute seem?*

- *How many times did your mind wander?*

These exercises can help you improve your concentration abilities and reduce beta brain waves. They are *not* necessarily relaxing. Contrary to the deep relaxation techniques, tongue relaxation,
and breathing practices we have already experienced in this chapter, concentration exercises can be stimulating and even somewhat
arousing. Therefore, do not practice them when your main goal is
one of psycho-physiological relaxation. Do practice them when you
would like to reduce the chatter in your mind and focus your concentration abilities.

INSIDE/OUTSIDE

A very important concept in the experience and understanding of
mastery is that of the connection between the inside and the outside. People of mastery are able to maintain an inner awareness at all

times and are also able to have an external awareness focused appropriately for the given situation. Opening up this channel between the inside and the outside is, in some ways, similar to opening up the channel between beta and delta. A flow of information is experienced, a connection, and ultimately a sense of awakening.

There are four different possibilities of this inside/outside awareness. Learning to have an understanding of which of these focuses you need for any given situation—and ultimately choosing consciously to create your experience in that level of awareness—is a major step toward mastery. The four possible categories are:

1. One-pointedness both inside and out—focusing on a spot inside to maintain the connection to yourself while at the same time focusing on a spot or a specific thing outside yourself. In this situation, you have narrow focus inside and narrow focus outside to create a sharp laser-like awareness emanating out of you toward the item of your concern.

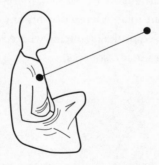

Figure 1: Internal Spot to External Spot

2. Or perhaps for some situations, you would prefer to have one-pointedness inside with expanded awareness outside. This is particularly useful for a time when you are facing an external challenge or danger and need to maintain sharp inner focus and groundedness while at the same time being aware of all external activities and possibilities.

Figure 2: Internal Spot to External Diffuse Awareness

3. Another possibility might be to have expanded inner awareness, encompassing all of your inner resources, while focusing with all of your concentration on one external object, situation, or idea. This might be particularly useful for a therapist interacting with a client, for anyone in an intense one-on-one communication, or for specific, focused problem-solving where you want to have access to all of your inner resources.

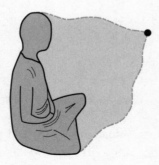

Figure 3: Diffuse Internal Awareness to External Spot

4. The final possibility is for you to have expanded inner awareness and expanded external awareness at the same time. Opening up

that wide of a channel of connection between the inside and the outside could explain some experiences of Attention Deficit Disorder (ADD), but it could also illustrate experiences of samadhi (total absorption in the object of meditation), cosmic consciousness, or bliss states (if the object of absorption is universal consciousness or God).

Figure 4: Diffuse Internal Awareness to Diffuse External Awareness

Ultimately, you want to be able to move back and forth freely and fluidly between these four different possibilities. It is also feasible, in mastery, to have more than one of these forms of awareness occurring simultaneously. Try practicing each of these four forms of awareness individually until you have a feel for the qualities and characteristics of each and how they differ. Then you might even want to try experiencing two or more at once. Make notes of which methods of awareness are most appropriate for which situations in your life. Again, you are developing mastery.

You will find this concept of simultaneously maintaining inside and outside awareness to be a constant source of support as you continue to develop mastery.

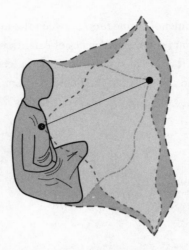

Figure 5: Four Forms of Awareness Simultaneously—Internal Spot, External Spot, Internal Diffuse Awareness, and External Diffuse Awareness

MASTERING BETA WITH IMAGERY

Images can also be used to master the beta contents of your mind. There are many types of thoughts that may occupy your mind unnecessarily, ranging from the irrelevant to the deeply stressful, or even to the positive, beneficial thoughts with inappropriate timing. Here are several imagery techniques that will help you master unwanted beta. You may also wish to try making up your own.

MASTERING BETA WITH IMAGERY

Imagine that you are holding a bunch of multi-colored, helium-filled balloons.

Anytime an unwanted thought comes through, place it in one of the balloons and let it go.

Watch it disappear into the distance.

You can choose the color of the balloon that you wish to place the thought in,

placing it into a red balloon, or a green, blue, yellow, or purple one.
Let the balloon go and watch it until it disappears completely.

■　■　■

Imagine now that you are walking out in the country on an autumn
  day.
Leaves are blowing all around you.
As you watch, you place any unwanted thought onto a leaf and
  watch it blow away.

■　■　■

Visualize the thoughts as gray clouds in a blue sky.
See this clearly.
Any thought that comes into your mind is a puff of gray cloud in an
  otherwise clear sky.
Gently begin to blow away the clouds with your breath.
Continue blowing the clouds away until the sky is completely blue
  and clear.

■　■　■

Occasionally there are thoughts in your mind with emotional
  content that you would like to eradicate completely.
Imagine writing these thoughts on a piece of paper,
then throwing the paper into a fire and burning it.
Notice what you feel as the thought burns up.

■　■　■

Sometimes you may have a creative thought or an important idea
  that keeps returning when you are trying to still your beta brain
  waves.

Because you don't want to lose the contents of this thought,
you allow it to continue to distract you.
If there is a thought in your mind that you would like to store in
   some way,
imagine writing this thought on a piece of paper,
then filing it away in a briefcase or filing cabinet
where you can store it to refer to later whenever you wish.

From these examples, you can see that there are many kinds of imagery that can be used to help you clear the contents of your mind, reduce beta waves, and still thought. We have used primarily visualization as the mode of imagery in these examples. In the next chapter, we will take a deeper look at not just visualization but also the other sensory images.

Now that you have learned the foundations of mastery, relaxing the body, and stilling the mind, it is time to focus on developing the gateway to meditation and the bridge to the subconscious mind, our alpha brain waves.

CREATING THE LINK
TO THE INNER SELF

Sensualization and the
Development of Alpha Waves

The very definition of *awakening* looked at through spiritual eyes implies *mastery*. Awakening implies an opening of the inner being that allows us a deeper access to ourselves and a broader knowledge and understanding of what we might call universal consciousness. The deepest profundity of this experience comes via our theta brain waves—the deep subconscious.

In order to reach the deep subconscious, we must open up the bridge to it—that intermediate ground in between waking and sleeping, that place of vivid, lucid imagery where we may be able to daydream happily for hours yet cannot seem to find when we most want control of it. It's a place of relaxation and peace, allowing detached awareness of *whatever is.*

Alpha brain waves, experienced by themselves without the addition of the wisdom of theta, give us a pleasant, light reverie that even on its own, can assist in creativity and insight. Alpha is where you have your most clear and distinct imagery. If theta is present, the origin, content, or meaning of the imagery may be personally significant, spiritually profound, or deeply moving. The theta gives the material, the context for the experience, but it is the alpha that provides the comprehensibility and lucidity.

Alpha is like a muscle you can exercise. Then, when you want it, you can turn it on at will to use in whatever way and context is appropriate at the time. We can exercise this muscle by practicing the very thing that alpha does best for us—sensory imagery.

The most commonly referred to form of sensory imagery is visualization. While visualization has been a helpful technique for many, the narrowness of the word itself has hindered the helpful use of sensory imagery in its fullest meaning. Visualization means to be able to create a mental picture using the visual sense. Many people have difficulty visualizing, partially because they believe that they have to *see* the image like a photograph, or, better yet, a movie, for it to be classed as a true visualization, and partially because their other senses may be more developed than their visual sense. They may be better at "tactilization" or at "audioization." In light of this, I call *all* sensory imagery, regardless of the sense or combination of senses involved, by the term **sensualization.**

Let's look first at visualization itself. Where do you experience your visual imagery? The majority of people experience their visual imagery somewhere in front of their eyes, as if it were projected on a movie screen in front of them or as if it were a "live action" around them. However, many people do not see visual imagery in this way. Other locations where imagery is "seen" are in the middle of the head behind the eyes, in the back of the head, outside the body in back or off to the sides, or even inside the body (not in the head)—in the heart, solar plexus, or stomach. It is also possible to have multiple visual fields in two or more distinct locations with two or more different imagery scenarios taking place at the same time. (I had a client who had one visual field for "yes" and another visual field for "no." The two fields changed size in accordance with the strength of each attitude. Another client "saw" images in the heart rather than "feeling" emotions.)

Many people "visualize" with a "sense of knowing" that the image is there. As long as they can describe it, tell you what color it is, and describe factors such as its shape, size, and position, I consider this "visualization" even without the ability to see the object.

When you visualize, are you outside the image looking in or inside the image looking out? You can be either. Some people experience the image as if they are in their own body using their senses in a very real way. When they see visual imagery, it is as if they are looking out of their own eyes at the images. Others see the image as if they are looking at themselves doing the activity. If the guided fantasy, for example, instructs them to take a walk along a country path, they *see themselves* walking along the path rather than just seeing the path stretched out in front of them, in which case to see themselves, they would have to look down at their feet.

Is one way better than the other? No. There are times when each has a function. If you want to use your imagery to make a change within yourself, the more you can experience it being inside you, the more effective your imagery will be. On the other hand, sometimes we use imagery to explore something that is dangerous or frightening, and if we were to experience it directly through the image, we would not be able to stay with it. By distancing ourselves from the image, we are better able to control our reaction to the experience and therefore work through the whole process.

It is even possible to "construct" a clear plexiglass wall between you and the image, creating a metaphorical safety wall between you and a scene too painful or dangerous to experience directly. This serves to give you a sense of security not present if you are "inside" or right next to the image. The optimum situation would be to have the ability to be both inside and outside the image at the same time. This may sound paradoxical, but not only is it possible, it is actually common for some people and is one aspect of mastery. **Once again we see the value of "inside/outside."**

Inside/Outside Visualization

Now imagine yourself walking along that country path.

Visualize the scene and see the vegetation on either side of the path.

See the colors and shapes.

Feel the textures with your fingers.

Notice the time of day, the weather, the temperature, the smells and sounds.

Experience this as if you are inside your own body "looking" out.

■ ■ ■

Now stop and start the exercise over.

This time see yourself walking down the country path.

Place yourself in the picture and look at yourself from the outside.

■ ■ ■

Allow yourself to reflect:

- *Was one of these methods easier than the other?*

- *Practice both so that they become familiar.*

- *See if you can combine the two.*

At first you may find yourself switching back and forth. Then the switching back and forth becomes more and more rapid. Finally, you experience both perspectives at the same time. Having the mental flexibility to move around within your imagery in this way will give you the maximum results when you wish to use your imagery to accomplish something.

ACCESS SENSE

We have what we can call an "access sense," the sense that is usually the strongest and appears first, heralding the arrival of the other senses. In other words, if I were to ask you to "hear a church bell ring," would you hear the sound first, or would you automatically see the image of a bell or the image of a church first and *then* hear the sound? Similarly, if I told you to taste a large, ripe strawberry, would you automatically see the fruit first before you even tried to taste it? If so, then your access sense is visual. Often we use it without realizing it, to activate the other senses in the imagery process.

Many people have an auditory, kinesthetic, or tactile access sense instead of a visual one and don't realize it—still hoping to see things first. Try the following exercise with your eyes closed.

DRINK SENSUALIZATION

Imagine that you are going to have a drink of some sort.
Is your beverage in a cup or a glass?
What color is the container, or is it transparent?
What color is the liquid?
Feel the container.
Is it hot or cold?
How full is the container?
Pick it up and feel the weight—but don't drink it yet.
Can you feel your elbow bend as you lift it up to smell it?
Put it back down on the table heavily with a bang?
(Try not to spill it, but if you sloshed it out, clean it up.)
Smell it.
Now finally, taste it. Be careful not to burn yourself if it is hot.
Drink as much as you want.
Open your eyes and take a few deep breaths.

Allow yourself to reflect:

- *What happened?*

- *What were you drinking?*

- *Could you see it?*

- *Could you feel the container with your hand as you held it?*

- *Could you tell the temperature?*

- *Could you feel your arm move or your elbow bend as you lifted it up?*

- *Could you smell it?*

- *Could you taste it?*

- *Did you hear the sound when you banged it back down on the table?*

- *Was it necessary to clean up a spill?*

If you can answer "yes" to any of these, you can "sensualize," even if you had trouble "seeing" it with the visual sense.

Practice the art of sensualization to increase the clarity and vividness of the material of the alpha waves. You will find that practicing sensualization not only helps you improve your sensualization ability, it also increases and improves alpha brain-wave production, increasing your access to that vital bridge to your subconscious mind. Practicing the kinds of imagery presented in the following exercise will develop a greater mental flexibility. The stronger the image you can evoke now using as many of your senses as possible, the more successful will be your outcome later, when the images you want to bring up come from a deeper and more meaningful place inside.

It is physiologically easier to produce alpha brain waves with your eyes closed. This is one of the main reasons that, in the initial stages of training mastery, I work with eyes-closed meditations. For the best results, practice these exercises while sitting or lying in a relaxed position with your eyes closed. You may wish to read them into a tape recorder so that you can listen to the instructions and keep your eyes closed throughout. Otherwise, read one instruction, then close your eyes and imagine it as clearly as possible. When your mind starts to wander or you feel your imagery is as complete and as "real" as it can be, open your eyes and read the next instruction. Later, we can learn to produce open-eyed alpha and even open-eyed awakened-mind states through gradually transferring that inner-oriented awakening to an external orientation similar to the concentration and focus exercises in the previous chapter (again, *inside/outside*).

SENSUALIZATION EXERCISE

VISUAL

- Begin by seeing as many colors as possible, not only the primary colors of red, yellow, and blue, but also the secondary colors of orange, green, and purple, and their various combinations, shades, tones, and tints—light blue, aqua, brown, pink, crimson, gold, peach, lilac. . . . Then add the opposites of black and white.

- Watch the clouds moving across a windy sky.

- See the vastness of thousands of stars in the sky on a summer's evening.

- Light a match in a darkened room.

- Standing on top of a high mountain, gaze over miles and miles of beautiful countryside below you.

- See a friend's face smiling at you.

- See the street your home is on, quickly passing each house until you get to your own front door.

- From your window seat in a landing airplane, see the city, the buildings, the streets, the cars, the airport, and finally the runway as you get closer and closer.

Allowing those images to fade, begin to *feel*.

TACTILE

- Feel soft fur under your fingers.

- Walking in the park, run your hand over the rough bark of a tree.

- Caress the soft smoothness of a baby's skin.

- Take ice cubes from the freezer and feel them melt in your hand.

- Wash your hands with soap and warm water.

- Experience the gritty feeling of brushing sand off your legs at the beach.

- Imagine the way your scalp feels as you comb or brush your hair.

- Feel a roughly cut plank of wood, but be careful of the splinters.

- Experience the cool air on your steaming body as you step out of the hot bath.

Allowing those images to fade, begin to hear:

AUDITORY

- The sound of a jet taking off.

- The whap of a tennis ball against the racket.

- Children laughing at the playground.

- The dentist's high-speed drill.

- The crackle of wood burning on an open fire.

- A foghorn echoing in the distance.

- The howl of a police siren.

- The dawn chorus of birds waking you in the early morning.

- Laughing voices, clattering cups, and tinkling glasses at a party.

Allowing those images to fade, begin to smell:

OLFACTORY

- The potent fumes you experience driving behind a truck.

- The smell of an outdoor barbeque.

- The soaps and lotions department in a store.

- The smell of a seafood market.

- The smell of burnt toast.

- Your favorite perfume or aftershave.

- Bread baking in a bakery.

- The smell of freshly brewed coffee.

- The smell of shoe polish as you are polishing your shoes.

- Lavender and roses.

Allowing those images to fade, begin to taste:

GUSTATORY

- The sharpness of pure lemon juice.

- The milky foam on a cup of cappuccino.

- A menthol cough drop.

- The salt on a potato chip.

- A bite of sharp cheese.

- A crisp, fresh apple.

- Cold vanilla ice cream melting in your mouth.

- A large, ripe strawberry.

- The minty freshness of toothpaste.

Allowing those images to fade, begin to experience:

KINESTHETIC

- The sensation of walking downstairs in the dark and feeling for the light.

- Reaching up on a high shelf for a container you can't see.

- Walking barefoot on a pebble beach.

- Playing tennis, baseball, volleyball, or your favorite sport.

- Dancing.

- Struggling to open a "childproof" medicine cap.

- Sunbathing or just lazing on a sheltered, deserted beach.

- Receiving a warm hug from an old friend.

Allowing those images to fade, now begin to put all of your senses
  together at once.
Sensualize what your life would be like if it were exactly as you
  wanted it to be.
What it would look like . . .
What it would feel like . . .
What it would sound like . . .
Even what it would smell and taste like . . .
. . . if your life were just the way you would like it to be.

■　■　■

When you are ready,
allow yourself to complete your imagery and return to the outside
  space,
opening your eyes and awakening alert and refreshed.

The following is a scale on which you can rate your experiences in
each of the categories of senses.

SENSUALIZATION SCALE

1. Lifelike imagery, as vivid and distinctive as the actual experience

2. Quite clear and well-defined imagery, representative of but not quite
   equal to the actual experience

3. Intermediate clarity but still realistic imagery

4. Hazy imagery with minimal representation of the actual experience

5. Formless, dim, indistinct, and unrecognizable

6. No imagery at all, only thinking of the experience

Allow yourself to reflect:

- *Take a few minutes to consider what you learned from these sensory imagery exercises.*

- *Which sense provided you with the most vivid experience?*

- *Which was the weakest?*

- *Did the strongest images all occur in one or two categories, or were they evenly spread throughout the senses?*

- *Did the strongest images come in brief flashes that disappeared as quickly as they came?*

- *Or were you able to maintain the vividness for a consistent period of time?*

- *Could you identify an access sense?*

Do not discount even the briefest imagery flashes. By recognizing even that split second of clarity, you can learn to lengthen it much more easily. Often, people will not recognize or admit to themselves that brief instant of insight when the experience was extremely lucid. They continue to think that they can't achieve clear mental imagery simply because *they are not able to maintain it.*

Sometimes, people are stuck in only one sense—frequently when this happens, it is visual. Notice when you tried to *hear* the bell ringing, did you *see* it instead? When you wanted to *smell* the bread, did you find yourself *looking* at a loaf? When you have one sense that is overpowering the others, you can use it as the foundation of your sensualization; you can build on it rather than stopping with it.

Try the Sensualization Exercise again, but this time use your strongest sense to help you access your weaker senses. In other words, if your strongest sense is visual and your weakest is auditory, see the bell before you hear it ring—but don't just stop at the "seeing." If your strongest sense is kinesthetic and your weakest is visual, feel yourself go through the motions of striking the match before you see the light flare up. If your strongest sense is auditory and your weakest is tactile, hear the sound of the ocean at the beach before you brush the sand off your legs. Play with these combinations of senses and images in any way that will help you improve the quality of your mental material. Remember that, ultimately, the more senses you can combine to create a vivid internal experience, the more productive and meaningful your sensualization will be.

Practicing the alpha development sensualization exercises can be helpful for more than just brain-wave development. For example, if you are an artist, seeing and feeling your art before you create it will greatly enhance your creative process. By sensualizing the next chapter that you are writing, you can unblock writer's block. By hearing the music, a composer understands the next movement. No matter what your creative medium—writing, painting, sculpture, music, cooking . . . the list is endless—you will improve your creative ability and productivity the more you are able to expand your sensualization repertoire. A master cook would have great difficulty if he or she were not able to sensualize what his or her dish would taste like with a little more salt added.

Sometimes using unexpected senses to create can have valuable as well as delightful consequences. In composing music, I have both danced it in order for the musician to play it from my movement and I have drawn it for the musician to play it from my picture. Imagery takes on a whole new meaning as we break down the barriers between the senses and build our sensualization abilities. I knew one musician who "tasted the difference between the colors of the notes" as he composed.

As potentially vivid and lucid as the sensualization exercises are, the personal meaning of the imagery may also appear somewhat mundane and ordinary. Good for producing alpha waves, they may not stimulate in you the theta production that comes from a deeper and more meaningful place inside. I have found that "spiritual sensualization imagery" can produce potentially stronger and more personally meaningful imagery. In fact, theta waves may also sometimes be stimulated if the image conjures up significant or profound impulses.

What follows is a series of spiritual images. In searching for the spiritual imagery of alpha, I found that the sensualizations were often evocative of various religions, not just nonsecular spirituality, because the imagery that re-creates those profound moments is often couched in religious tradition. For the most part in this book, I stay away from any particular religious focus, accepting all routes into spirituality and mastery. However, in this exercise, I do just the opposite, intentionally drawing on the religious to create spiritual imagery. Some images may be familiar to you, some may not. Some images may feel comfortable, some may "push buttons." Take this as an exercise in imagery, and allow yourself to see what happens.

SPIRITUAL SENSUALIZATION EXERCISE

VISUAL

- A thousand-petal lotus

- Flickering candlelight

- Flame of burning fire

- Image of Christ on the crucifix

- Gleaming golden Quan Yin

- Temple filled with incense smoke

- Light flooding through stained-glass windows in a cathedral

- Smiling Buddha

TACTILE

- The feel of *mala* beads in your hands
- The rosary
- Striking the match to light the menorah
- Communion wafer melting in your mouth

GUSTATORY

- The taste of communion wine
- Japanese tea at the end of the tea ceremony
- Ambrosia and nectar

OLFACTORY

- The smell of incense burning
- Frankincense and myrrh

AUDITORY

- The crackle of the Yule log
- The sound of Gregorian chants
- Deep tones of organ music
- Church bells ringing
- Tibetan bowls

KINESTHETIC

- Clasping your hands in prayer
- Sensation of kneeling

- Sufi dancing and whirling

- The felt sense of the kundalini serpent coiled at the base of your spine

- The sensation of rocking as energy moves through your body

And finally . . .
The felt sense of your higher power, God, universal consciousness, or divine energy in whatever form it takes.

Again refer back to the Sensualization Scale on page 63.

Allow yourself to reflect:

- *Did these images stimulate a stronger or a weaker experience?*

- *Was your access sense the same or different?*

- *Did any particular image affect you in an unexpected way?*

- *What did you learn about yourself from this exercise?*

As you are developing your imagery ability, you are improving your alpha brain-wave production. This means that you are improving the bridge to your subconscious mind. The more you practice, the better your abilities for recalling theta contents will become. This will also improve dream recall, meditation recall, and memory access.

The following is a word picture or sensualization that will help you both develop alpha brain waves and at the same time build your sensory imagery ability. Read it through before closing your eyes and sensualizing.

ALPHA DEVELOPMENT WORD PICTURE

Sensualize yourself walking down a narrow country lane on a warm, sunny afternoon. To your left is a valley stretching far into the distance—a patchwork of greens and browns, fading into purple at the horizon, where the hills meet the blue of the sky. To your right is a leafy hedge-bank of dark green, and dotted here and there are the bright summer colors of blue flowers, golden buttercups, and the fallen petals of an overhanging wild cherry tree. The lane stretches into the distance in front of you and finally disappears, swerving gradually to the left.

Far in the distance you begin to hear a train approaching, and you look to see the tracks in the valley below just as the engine comes into sight. You watch and listen as it passes through the length of the valley. The sound grows louder at first then begins to fade. For a few moments after the train has disappeared from sight, you can still hear the soft rumbling growing fainter and fainter in the distance, and then you are left with the quiet stillness of a peaceful summer day; the occasional mooing of cows grazing on the hillside, the buzz of a nearby bee darting round a delicate pink-centered flower—and from a distant meadow comes the bleating of sheep and the barking of a farmer's dog.

Up ahead there appears to be a break in the hedge on your right, and when you approach, you see it is an old, rusty iron gate. It is too high to look over, and the vines covering it prevent you from looking through. You try the latch and it is open, so you push. But it only opens an inch or two. You push a little harder this time, and the gate begins to swing open, creaking loudly on its rusty hinges.

You pass through the gate, and there stretching out in front of you is a beautiful garden of brilliant-colored flowers of all varieties and vivid green leaves. As you walk along the path in front of you, you stop to smell the scent of the roses and feel the softness of their petals. Up ahead you come to a large, round pond. Stopping to look, you see the brilliant flash of goldfish—quite large ones—darting about in the pool among the lily pads floating on the top.

You make your way across the garden, stopping here to smell a flower, there to feel the grass and to gaze at the one fluffy white cloud in the sky. Following first one path and then another, you lose yourself in the beauty of this unforeseen moment. Until eventually up ahead you see another old, rusty iron gate—but it looks like the same one! Running the last few steps through the garden, you reach the gate and pull it open—and you find yourself back outside on the gentle country lane. Nearby, a blackbird is stirring, and the valley stretches into the distance as you continue your afternoon walk.

BEINGNESS MEDITATIONS

One avenue for developing sensory imagery abilities while at the same time building alpha-production skills is to imagine that you are some other kind of being or object and "live the experience" of that being using as many senses as possible. Read the following through, and then begin the practice after a few minutes of relaxation and beta mastery.

ANIMAL SENSUALIZATION

Sensualize yourself as some kind of animal.
It could be a real animal or a fantasy animal.
If you have trouble identifying what you are, look down at your feet.
What kind of feet . . . or hooves . . . or claws . . . do you have?

What is your skin covering?
How big are you?
What is your shape?

How do you move?
What do you eat?
Where do you live?

What kind of sound do you make?
How do you communicate?
Do you live alone . . . with a mate . . . in a group?

What makes you happy . . . ?
                        sad . . . ?
                        afraid . . . ?
                        strong and powerful . . . ?
What gives you courage?

Live the experience of being this animal for a few minutes.
Sensualize it using as many senses as possible.

You may wish to refer to the Sensualization Scale on page 63 to ground your imagery.

"Kick Starting" Your Alpha Brain Waves

Following is a physiological mechanism that can be used as a way to actually "kick start" your alpha. It is a simple but profound technique for accessing alpha brain waves.

Producing alpha waves is physiologically linked to your eyes. If you close your eyes, you will produce stronger alpha more quickly than if you keep them open. **If you roll your eyes upward in your head, you will produce alpha even more.**

Alpha Eye Rolls

With your eyes closed, inhale and gently raise your eyes to look toward the center of your forehead.

When you exhale, lower your eyes.
Again when you inhale, gently raise your eyes behind closed
    eyelids.
And when you exhale, lower your eyes again.
Repeat for three or four more breaths.
(Note: Do not strain your eyes. If you feel any discomfort, stop imme-
diately.)

Now try it this way:
With your eyes closed, exhale and gently raise your eyes to look
    toward the center of your forehead.
When you inhale, lower your eyes again.
When you exhale, gently raise your eyes.
When you inhale, lower your eyes.
Repeat for three or four more breaths.

Most people find the first method more natural and therefore
more effective. However, a few find the second method extraordi-
narily effective. Try both and you will know which works best
for you.

I suggest you use this exercise sparingly. After a few minutes, its
alpha-producing quality diminishes as a form of habituation occurs.
It is the movement of the eye roll that causes the alpha flare—not
holding the eyes continuously up. The eye muscles are delicate and
easy to tire, and creating eyestrain would be counterproductive to
what you are trying to do. A few breaths—five to ten at the most—at
the beginning of the meditation would be most effective. Even three
would be quite sufficient.

Remember, the production of alpha waves opens up the bridge
so that you have access to the flow of information between the subconscious and the conscious minds. Consider a reaction that you
might have when you are trying to remember something. *You look
up!* Rolling your eyes upward is often an automatic response the
body makes when trying to access lost or hidden information. You

naturally open up the alpha bridge so that, *if the information is there,* it can come to you more easily.

The masters have also long used the eye rolling upward as an integral part of some of their meditation techniques. No one needs to tell them it assists in activating alpha brain waves; they intuitively understand that it more quickly contributes to the altered and higher states of consciousness accessed in meditation.

Now we will move on to look at the brain-wave component of the meditation state that provides the depth, profundity, and spirituality of the experience—the theta brain waves. Here is where mastery really begins to come into its own. The territory of theta is a land that the masters have long known how to navigate. Let us continue our journey there.

ACCESSING AND
EXPERIENCING THE DEEP

Developing Theta Brain Waves

What truly differentiates an **awakened mind** from the mind of
the ordinary individual is his or her capacity to be in conscious contact with the deepest and most profound aspects of the
inner being. Accessed through theta brain waves, these ordinarily
subconscious parts of the mind hold the key to creativity, insight,
spiritual awareness, and a variety of expressions of mastery.

The *content* of theta brain waves only remains subconscious
when there is no alpha present simultaneously to provide the link to
the conscious mind. When you are producing the classic meditation brain-wave pattern of alpha and theta, you can get in touch with
the most profound depths as well as have the vividness and clarity of
imagery provided by the alpha to transmit this experience in a tangible way so that the conscious thought process of beta can inter-
pret it, understand it, and act upon it.

Let's begin by looking at the range of experiences that this addition of theta can bring to the meditator. It may seem peculiar
that, in one breath, I can associate the height of personal mastery

and intensely spiritual states with the depth of unresolved psychological material and inner subconscious wounds and imply that they come from the same "place." But, in fact, that is exactly what I am saying.

The theta brain waves can be the repository of years of "unfinished business." The fact that we have this "stuff" lodged in our subconscious minds may actually provide one of the biggest impediments to our personal evolution and natural development of mastery, because the mind plays games with itself to spare itself the effort and potential pain of releasing this material and making room for more creative and spiritual content.

If we have something painful lodged deep inside, it is possible that the alpha brain waves retreat or diminish to protect the conscious thought process from being aware of this subconscious content. If I look carefully at the EEG of certain clients, I can actually see the subconscious content being hidden—scurrying away as we get closer—not wishing to reveal itself. Is it any wonder then that awakening the mind continues to elude us, if we are constantly averting our gaze from our inner wounds?

Only through the *full and complete access of theta* can we truly attain mastery. And since theta is the subconscious, we must allow ourselves to open to the possibility not only of releasing any unfinished business but also of quickly healing it so that we can move on, leaving room for the profound spiritual content that is also available through theta.

I am *not* saying that it is necessary to go through years of therapy, or indeed any therapy, to attain this clarity. Neither is it necessary to completely understand, remember, or make logical sense of the material that may be blocking the development of the subconscious. If that material is negative or in the form of a wound, what is significant is that it be released and/or healed. In fact, those two are fairly synonymous—the healing may come through the release or the release may come through the healing.

In order to awaken our minds, we must clear access to the subconscious and develop the theta brain waves in conjunction with the alpha brain waves so that the flow of information between the conscious and the unconscious mind can be encouraged and developed.

It is also important to say that as we begin to access and develop the theta brain waves, we do not anticipate difficulty. *Whatever* we find there is valid and valuable. We are just as likely to find suppressed creativity, long-forgotten insights, or a true sense of spiritual awareness as we are to find wounds to heal. The first key is to value and validate any material you access *without judgment.* The second key is to realize that anything you find in your subconscious *can be acknowledged, understood and transformed if appropriate.*

You have the ability to go inside and make conscious changes, to heal, to open, to transform, and to evolve your innermost being.

In light of this, I would like to introduce a theta-accessing meditation that is designed to help you develop and begin to gain mastery of this most important inner place. Please remember that this is *your* meditation. If you come upon a place inside that you don't feel ready to open, that is absolutely fine. Leave it till another day, or simply give it your blessings and move on.

House of Doors

Let your mind clear, and focus on your breathing.
(Please spend at least five to ten minutes relaxing before continuing. You may wish to refer back to the foundations of relaxing the body and stilling the mind in Chapter One as preparation for this meditation.)

And now, from this place of deep relaxation and peace,
In your mind, create an environment.
Imagine or create an environment outdoors, somewhere pleasant
    for you.
It could be the mountains, the country, the beach . . .
Sensualize it . . .
Walk around it in your mind.
Explore this environment carefully, using as many senses as
    possible.
Experience the colors, the shapes, the textures, the sounds, the
    smells . . . even the tastes of this environment.
Notice the time of day . . . the atmosphere . . . the
    temperature . . .
Feel it with your mind.
Make any changes that you would like to make in this environment
    to make it safe and secure for you.

■　　■　　■

Now, within this environment, place a house.
Don't go inside yet; just see it from the outside.
You're going to go on a journey through this house.
So, going in through the front door . . .
And passing through an entrance hallway . . .
You find yourself in a room covered in mirrors.
Mirrors all around you . . . on all of the walls . . .
And you notice your image . . . your reflection . . . in these
    mirrors.

Now, passing through the room of mirrors,
You find yourself in a long hallway.
A seemingly endless corridor with rows of doors on either side.
And each of the doors is a different color.

You begin to walk down this hallway, passing door . . . after
  door . . . after door . . .
Until you come to stop in front of a door on your left.
You notice the color of the door.
And on the door, there may be a label, a symbol, or an image.
If so, you see it and understand.
When you are ready, you open this door and go into the room that is
  behind it.
Take all of the time that you need to very thoroughly explore this
  room and its contents.

■ ■ ■

While you are in this room, you have the power to make any
  changes that you want.
Take the time now to make any changes you wish to make within
  this room.

■ ■ ■

In a few moments, you are going to leave this room.
So allow yourself to take the time now to complete anything that
  you are doing here.
You can always return at any time if you would like to spend more
  time here.

And now, when you are ready, leave this room behind and go back
  out into the corridor.
Close the door behind you, but don't lock it, so that you can return
  if you wish.
And continue your way on down the hallway, again passing door
  after door . . .
Until you come to stop in front of a door on your right.
Again, notice the color of the door . . .
. . . and the label or symbol, if there is one.

When you are ready, open this door and explore what is behind it.
Take as long as you need to very thoroughly explore this space.

■ ■ ■

Remember that you have the power to make any changes that you
   want to make within this place.

■ ■ ■

Now, when you are ready, begin to allow yourself to come to
   completion with whatever you are doing . . .
Remember that you can always return here if you wish.

And now, leave this room behind.
Go back out into the corridor, close the door behind you, but don't
   lock it, so that you can return if you wish . . .
And this time, retrace your steps back down the hallway the way
   you came . . .
Back past the first door that you entered.
Back into the room of mirrors.
Notice any changes in your reflection . . . your image.
Back through the entrance hallway.
Back out the front door.
Back into your environment.
Making any changes that you want to make within your
   environment, find a comfortable place to sit . . . and to meditate.
Meditate on what you experienced in the house of doors . . .
And what it might mean to you.

■ ■ ■

When you are ready,
Find a few "keys" or "landmarks" to bring back with you when you
   reawaken,

To remind you of where you have been, what you have experienced,
   and what you have gained from that experience.
These keys may be images, symbols, body sensations, colors,
   emotions, words, or phrases . . .
Anything that will help you remember your experience . . .
. . . even tastes, smells, sounds, and textures that were present in
   your meditation.

In your own time, when you are ready, begin to allow yourself to
   find a closure for your meditation.
In your own time, when you are ready, begin to allow yourself to
   return . . .
Back to the outside space.
Allow yourself to reawaken and return
Feeling alert . . .
. . . and refreshed.

Take several deep, rapid breaths,
And allow yourself to stretch, beginning with fingers and toes.
When you are ready, open your eyes and reenter the outside space.

Allow yourself to reflect:

- *What happened in the two rooms you entered?*

- *Did you make any changes?*

- *Were you able to see yourself in the mirrors? (If not, next
  time try looking at your feet first in the mirror, and then
  work your way upward.)*

- *Was your image in the mirrors on the way out of the house
  different from your image in the mirrors on the way in?*

- *What changed?*

- *Was there a room you didn't like, couldn't see, or were unable to gain access to?*

- *What did you learn about yourself in this process?*

This meditation is a generic theta-accessing meditation designed to help you access **whatever is on top or most important or most available for you right now in your subconscious.**

Every time you open a door, you are opening a door into the subconscious.

You can do this meditation an infinite number of times and still benefit from it, as there are an infinite number of doors available to open.

GROUNDING THE EXPERIENCE

When you do this meditation, you might want to have a pencil and paper handy. You have probably had a number of experiences within this meditation that will

a. give you information about yourself, and

b. help you remember what the meditation state of consciousness felt like, so that you can re-create these experiences and return to this state more easily next time. You may also have some unfinished business in the house that you would like to go back and finish in a subsequent meditation.

Because the nature of meditation brain waves is to be near or below the conscious border, meditators—especially those with less experience—tend to lose or forget the content of the exercise very easily. Remembering details of the experience will help build the ability to meditate in the future, reinforcing this state as a familiar brain-wave pattern.

So how do we bring back content? If you have been producing a true meditation pattern of theta and alpha, you will have already created the bridge that has allowed you to be aware of the content of the experience while it was happening. This is why creating the environment is so important at the beginning of the meditation. The more clearly you can sensualize the initial environment, the more you will encourage your alpha brain waves to create the bridge to your subconscious mind.

If your alpha is low in frequency, however, the material will only travel partially along that bridge. Because no higher frequencies are drawing it strongly enough toward consciousness, it will literally turn around and slide back down into the subconscious. In these cases, you *know* that you had the experience, and it even feels as if it is there on the tip of your tongue, but you can't quite get it to emerge from the subconscious.

What you need is a tool to bring your experience into full conscious awareness immediately after you emerge from the meditation state. To bring it all the way up into your beta waves, you must put it into thought form. The best way to do this is through words. Writing or speaking about the experience immediately after you have completed it will draw the contents up into your beta mind so that you can retain them consciously.

If you are practicing this meditation alone, you may put your experience into words by writing it down (or speaking it out loud into a tape recorder, so that you have a record of it). Write down your "keys" first. Then go back and fill in the details. Recount as many particulars as possible. The more minute observations you can remember, the more the meditation will stay with you.

If you are practicing these meditations with a friend or in a group, you can describe the experiences to one another. Don't analyze or discuss the meaning at any length until everyone has had a chance to make his or her content fully conscious. If you talk (using your beta waves) about someone else's experience before you report on yours, you are likely to lose your own content because analyzing their story may break the link from your conscious mind to your experience in your own subconscious mind. Sometimes that link is so tenuous that the effort of activating your beta waves for discussion will pull you out of your alpha and theta, and the details of your own experience may fade. After everyone has had a chance to share at least their keys and landmarks, then you can discuss freely and interact without fear of losing your own experience.

HOW DOES WRITING DOWN KEY WORDS OR IMAGES HELP YOU RETURN TO THE MEDITATION STATE?

Meditation involves a "felt sense," a combination of sensations experienced on many different levels. By using your beta brain waves to verbalize and make conscious the different ingredients and sensory experiences you had during your meditation, you will have a greater access both to its content and to "how it feels" to be in a meditative state.

Keys and landmarks can be state-oriented or content-oriented. Although I often use the words interchangeably, I tend to think of landmarks as related to state—as in the Table of Subjective Landmarks in Chapter One. Keys I relate more to content, words, or symbols that can remind you how to unlock the meaning hidden in the subconscious mind.

The next time you want to meditate, sit down and remember the felt sense of the landmarks to reenter the state of meditation and the keys to access the content of theta. By making use of the landmarks or keys that drew up the experience of your subconscious mind to your conscious mind, you can simply reverse the route and ride them back down again. You can find yourself once again in meditation. You have opened up the channels. The more you now use these channels—deepen them, broaden them, and strengthen them—the easier it will become for you to reenter meditation at will, and the quicker you will experience mastery.

DEALING WITH THE CONTENT

There are many principles you can use in dealing with the material that arises from the theta waves. If you are confronting hidden traumas and feel you are getting in over your head, I urge you to seek the help of a good counselor or mental-health practitioner. Please be conscientious in your choice of therapist. When looking for an appropriate and helpful adviser, you will probably find that the sensitivity level, personal integrity, experience, and spiritual evolution of the individual that you choose is often much more important than the technique they use. Getting proper support while you are healing painful subconscious material may be helpful to assure that the process is effective, lasting, and safe. Otherwise, consider the following ideas as you work on your own transformation:

Don't Be Afraid of the Content. Whatever appears is part of you, and as such, deserves to be respected and even loved no matter what it is.

You Can Always Make Changes Inside. Nothing is permanent or fixed about these images and the inner states they represent. You can take this information and act upon it.

You Don't Have to Do the Work All at Once. Understanding, healing, transforming, and integrating your issues may take time.

You Can Always Return. If you found these images once, you can find them again. Try to leave markers or find keys to help you reenter the state of consciousness where you found the content that you want to revisit.

Nothing Is Too Overwhelming or Too Painful to Eventually Be Healed. Perseverance and willingness to heal have a remarkable effect on the subconscious.

If You Don't Find Anything "Significant," Don't Worry. Some people are afraid that they are not really in theta unless they are experiencing something deep, meaningful, or difficult. Absolutely not! Theta can be a place of quiet contemplation and rest. Also, what may seem to have no significance to you now may prove to be very important to you later. Often, the smallest baby step provides the impetus for the crucial turning point.

Develop Your Spirituality. Creating or strengthening a conscious connection with whatever divine source or higher power you believe in will give you limitless resources for healing, growing, and grounding in your theta.

Keys to Accessing Theta

The key to accessing theta is to find a way to go deeply into yourself—into your own subconscious. The types of images that best access theta brain waves are those that take you on long journeys that ultimately take you very deep inside. The actual image itself doesn't matter; it is the effect the image has on your brain waves that is important. Images that take you down, through, and in help to access theta brain waves. The more *changes* you make, the deeper you tend to go. Remember the experience in the House of Doors meditation on page 76. After helping stimulate alpha waves with the sensual imagery in the outdoor environment, you went *in through* the front door, *passing through* an entrance hallway, *into* and *through* a room of mirrors, *down* a long hallway, *opening* a door, and going *through* the doorway, *into* a room. Then the process deepened your brain waves even more by repeating it on the opposite side of the hall.

You can also use images that take you *under, over, around,* and *up* to help deepen theta waves. You can create your own theta-accessing meditation by developing imagery using these directional movements.

Some examples:

Allow yourself to go . . .

- *down* stairs.

- *down* and *around* a long spiral staircase.

- *under* an archway.

- *into* a tunnel and down deep *into* the ground.

- *along* a narrow passageway.

- *through* a big, wrought-iron gate.

- *up* a steep incline.

- *inside* a large square structure.

- *over* a pile of bricks that is blocking a hidden sanctuary.

- *beneath* the hanging crystal.

- *into* the exact center of an octagonal space.

(. . . where you will find the answer you have been seeking.)

Once you have arrived at the end of your journey, you need to have something to meditate about. It is good to set an expectation that you will experience or find something valuable once you arrive in that state.

This expectation accomplishes two things: It gives you a structure around which to meditate—something on which to lean—and it offers you an opportunity to experience content in your subconscious, thereby building *more* theta waves. If you just arrive at the end of your journey and do nothing further, you might still continue to produce some theta, but you might also stop producing theta as soon as you stop your journey. Having some sort of content at the end of your journey gives your theta waves something on which to focus. This content in turn stimulates more theta waves, allowing you to continue to learn something about your own inner workings. This process of self-discovery cannot take place unless you continue to produce theta waves in proper balance with your other brain waves.

In this chapter, we are interested primarily in accessing *any* theta and developing our ability to be in the subconscious state while retaining a link (alpha) to the conscious mind (beta). In later chapters, we will look at accessing particular content for specific purposes, such as self-healing, creative inspiration, or spiritual development.

What Kind of Content Should I Use?

The content can be specific to a particular situation or question in your life, or it can be general and simply focused on a broad category. Examples of specific contents might be:

- deciding which of the two job offers to accept

- solving the design problem on the drawing board at work

- handling a delicate communication problem with your spouse

- finding money for the Christmas presents

- passing your final exam

- writing the magazine article

- healing a trauma experienced in early childhood

The possibilities are endless. If you are seeking the answer to a specific question, however, you must guard against using beta to solve your problem. Chapter Four will show you how to add beta to your meditation pattern for the specific purpose of problem solving. Then you can look at these detailed questions with your conscious and subconscious minds connected.

However, to develop theta without the addition of beta, you might prefer to choose nonspecific or general content. These types of general topics might include:

- personal healing

- finding stillness and serenity

- inner security

- higher self

- increased awareness

- creativity

- compassion

- love

- God

- healing others

- universal peace

- awakening

The topics are endless, so it is best to choose a general area in advance. Sit down, close your eyes, and get ready to begin, but before you still your mind and empty it of beta waves, think about what you would like to focus your meditation on. If you have a specific question or problem like those listed first, set an intention that you will get some information or guidance during your meditation. *Then forget it!* Let it go completely, and begin your meditation. If you have a generic topic, again, focus on that idea for a few moments, then let it go.

Later, when you complete your journey down and get to the place of stillness and meditation, let the insight or experience you are seeking well up from your subconscious theta waves. Don't analyze, think about, or even try to understand what you are experiencing. You can save that for later, when you ground the meditation back in your beta waves.

The Difference Between
Alpha Imagery and Theta Imagery

When images appear within your mind, they may have a variety of qualities and characteristics that can help indicate their origin within your consciousness. Understanding the difference between alpha images and theta images can help you not only determine your brain-wave pattern without the use of an EEG but also help you understand the meaning and significance of the content.

Images generated by alpha waves are clearer, sharper, and usually more vivid than those generated by theta waves. The colors are stronger and more varied. The edges are cleaner. Images generated by pure alpha are also less meaningful and do not seem to be coming from deep within you. They are also easier to create on command.

In contrast, images generated by theta waves are usually darker, fuzzier, and less distinct. They can be intensely personally meaningful and feel as if they are coming from the very depths of your being. Or they can feel as if they are divine inspiration, a gift from some sort of higher power. Sometimes, they seem to be surrounded in light. A sense of "knowing" can accompany them—knowing that this is the truth, knowing that this is the right action to take, knowing that you have touched something important inside. But don't always expect clear insight and moments of illumination from your theta waves. You can also swim around in your subconscious as if it were a murky swamp of perplexing obscurity.

Sometimes, theta imagery will be preceded or accompanied by washes of blue or purple colors, a flare of blue or purple light, or even a blue "dot" in the center of your inner field of vision. These signify a strong flare of theta waves. Have you ever heard the saying, "It came to me out of the blue"?

Following is a generic theta-accessing meditation that can be used for any purpose you wish. If you would like to contact a specific kind of content, simply have the intention in advance that you will find what you are looking for at the end.

The Down and In Meditation

Let your mind clear and focus on your breathing.
(*Please spend at least five to ten minutes relaxing before continuing. You may wish to refer back to the foundations of relaxing the body and stilling the mind in Chapter One as preparation for this meditation.*)

And as you move deeper into your meditation, you have a sense of
    going down a well . . .
Continuing to go down, deep into the subconscious . . .

Down . . .

A feeling of moving downstairs . . .
and through long corridors . . .
Twisting and turning . . .
Through archways and strange circular doorways . . .
Always going down . . .

Sometimes the grade is steep,
Sometimes only a slight decline,
But always going down . . .

As you move through the tunnels and corridors of your mind,
you may see beautiful iridescent lights of all colors . . .

The atmosphere changes—sometimes hot, sometimes cool,
    sometimes damp, sometimes dry, sometimes misty, sometimes
    clear . . .
Frequently, there are open doorways, passages, and corridors that
    you could enter but decide not to . . .
You see lights and hear sounds coming from these places, some
    inviting and some perhaps disturbing . . .
But still you move on . . .

■   ■   ■

Something from very deep down within you is beckoning you . . .
Something important . . . somehow familiar, but you don't know
    what it is . . .
You are being irrevocably drawn toward this mystical place.

And now you see the end of your journey . . .
The end of your path . . .
There before you is the place to which you have been traveling,
That mystical, magical place that is so important for you that you
    have kept going to get there against all odds.

Find out now what this place is, why it is important for you, what
    there is to learn here, and why you are drawn here.

Perhaps you will have a vision . . .
or receive insight . . .

Perhaps it is for a spiritual connection . . .

Perhaps for healing . . .

Perhaps simply a sense of well-being and peace inside . . .

Allow yourself to receive what it is that your subconscious is
 seeking to give you . . .

And take all the time you need to do this, beginning now . . .

■　　■　　■

In your own time, when you are ready, begin to allow yourself to
 return . . .
Back to the outside space.
Allow yourself to reawaken and return
Feeling alert . . . and refreshed.

Take several deep, rapid breaths,
And allow yourself to stretch, beginning with fingers and toes.
When you are ready, open your eyes and reenter the outside
 space.

There are many ways down into the theta state, from the detailed, specific journey described in the House of Doors meditation,
to the more generalized images in the Down and In Meditation. I
would like to give you one more theta meditation, this time for the
specific purpose of healing.

HEALING CIRCLE

Allow yourself to take some time to relax your body . . .
And still your mind.

■ ■ ■

There is almost a sense of moving backward,
Backward into softness,
Backward into warmth,
Falling . . .
Falling quickly now, faster and faster into a deep meditation . . .
And the faster you fall,
the more relaxed you become.

As you fall, you are aware of passing through different levels of
    consciousness.
They may be presented to you as images, sights, sounds, voices,
    body sensations, feelings, even smells and tastes . . .
And you fall beyond them . . .

Now you begin to slow.
Still you are falling, but gently, much more slowly . . .
almost . . . drifting down.
And down below you . . .
far, far down below you . . .
you see a circle . . .
And it is toward the exact center of this circle that you are
    falling . . .
A healing circle . . .
Getting closer and closer now,
And the closer you get, the slower you are falling,
And you see that it is a healing circle,
the very center of which you are moving toward,
Now hovering just above it.

And with exquisite gentleness and softness . . .
You come to rest
in the exact center of this circle

So that you are lying symmetrically in the center of the healing
   circle
that you can see or feel very clearly all around you.
And the healing begins . . .

It may take many forms.
You may feel strange and pleasurable sensations . . .
And as the healing permeates your body,
there may be messages that come to you, or just an indication of
   where the next step on your path may lead you.

And now, ever so gently, you feel yourself rise out of your physical
   body
into your spirit body,
your higher self,
And the healing continues
and becomes even stronger
as it is directed to your spirit body . . .
And it feels good.

■   ■   ■

And now, as your higher self begins to feel whole and full,
you descend again . . .
Passing through the emotional and mental bodies,
Cleansing them as you move through.
Back into the physical body once again,
Taking into the physical body all the healing that you received in
   your higher self,
Integrating that healing into the physical body,
Feeling yourself aligned, integrated, and in harmony within yourself.
At peace.

■   ■   ■

In your own time, when you are ready, begin to allow yourself to
   return . . .
Back to the outside space.
Allow yourself to reawaken and return
Feeling alert . . .
and refreshed.

Take several deep, rapid breaths,
And allow yourself to stretch, beginning with fingers and toes.
When you are ready, open your eyes and reenter the outside
   space.

Again be aware of the *entry* into the theta state. You could use
the first part of this meditation to open up your theta brain waves to
any of the generalized topics listed on page 87.

For example, to substitute *peace* for *healing,* the meditation
might read like the following. Please note that I have <u>underlined</u> all
of the changes that I made to the original meditation.

Circle of Peace

Allow yourself to take some time to relax your body . . .
And still your mind.

■   ■   ■

There is almost a sense of moving backward
Backward into softness,
Backward into warmth,
Falling . . .
Falling quickly now, faster and faster into a deep meditation,
And the faster you fall,
the more relaxed you become.

As you fall, you are aware of passing through different levels of
    consciousness.
They may be presented to you as images, sights, sounds, voices,
    body sensations, feelings, even smells and tastes . . .
And you fall beyond them . . .

Now you begin to slow.
Still you are falling, but gently, much more slowly . . .
almost . . . drifting down.
And down below you . . .
far, far down below you . . .
you see a circle . . .
And it is toward the exact center of this circle that you are falling . . .
A <u>circle of peace</u> . . .
Getting closer and closer now,
And the closer you get, the slower you are falling,
And you see that it is a <u>circle of peace</u>,
the very center of which you are moving toward,
Now hovering just above it.

And with exquisite gentleness and softness . . .
You come to rest
in the exact center of this circle
So that you are lying symmetrically in the center of the <u>peace</u> circle
that you can see or feel very clearly all around you
And <u>you can feel this peace begin to enter you . . .</u>

It may take many forms.
You may feel strange and pleasurable sensations . . .
And as the <u>peace</u> permeates your body,
there may be messages that come to you, or just an indication of
    where the next step on your path may lead you.

And now, ever so gently, you feel yourself rise out of your physical
    body

into your spirit body,
your higher self,
And the <u>peace</u> continues <u>to permeate you</u>
and becomes even stronger
as it is directed to your spirit body . . .
<u>Peace . . . entering your spirit . . .</u>
And it feels good.

■　■　■

And now, as your higher self <u>truly begins to feel peaceful,</u>
you descend again . . .
Passing through the emotional and mental bodies,
<u>Bringing them peace</u> as you move through.
Back into the physical body once again,
Taking into the physical body all the <u>peace</u> you received in your
    higher self,
Integrating that <u>peace throughout . . .</u>
Feeling yourself aligned, integrated, and in harmony within
    yourself.
At peace.

■　■　■

When you are ready, close and ground your meditation as you did
    for the Healing Circle.

Although the concepts of healing and peace are very similar,
they are not the same. You may want to use the Healing Circle if you
are ill and in need of healing, whereas the concept of a Circle of
Peace might be better utilized when you would simply like to meditate for a sense of inner serenity and tranquility, and it could easily
be practiced at the end of a tiring or stressful day.

Note that by simply changing just a few words, you can alter the focus and therefore the result of the experience deep within your subconscious. In a similar way, you can tailor any meditation in this book to better suit your specific needs. Let's look at how you could change the same meditation slightly more concretely to get yet a different focus.

CREATIVITY CIRCLE

Allow yourself to take some time to relax your body . . .
And still your mind.

■ ■ ■

There is almost a sense of moving backward,
Backward into softness,
Backward into warmth,
Falling . . .
Falling quickly now, faster and faster into a deep meditation,
And the faster you fall,
the more relaxed you become.

As you fall, you are aware of passing through different levels of
    consciousness.
They may be presented to you as images, sights, sounds, voices,
    body sensations, feelings, even smells and tastes . . .
And you fall beyond them . . .

Now you begin to slow.
Still you are falling, but gently, much more slowly . . .
almost . . . drifting down.
And down below you . . .
far, far down below you . . .
you see a circle . . .

And it is toward the exact center of this circle that you are falling . . .
A <u>creativity</u> circle . . .
Getting closer and closer now,
And the closer you get, the slower you are falling,
And you see that it is a <u>creativity</u> circle,
the very center of which you are moving toward,
Now hovering just above it.

And with exquisite gentleness and softness . . .
You come to rest
in the exact center of this circle
So that you are lying symmetrically in the center of the <u>creativity</u>
     circle,
<u>And you can begin to have a sense of creativity around you and</u>
     <u>within you . . .</u>

<u>This creative inspiration</u> may take many forms.
<u>You may see images . . .</u>
<u>Or hear words . . .</u>
<u>Or feel body sensations . . .</u>
<u>Or it may be just a sense of "knowing" . . .</u>

<u>Knowing what it is that you need to do,</u>
<u>Or understanding what is possible</u>
<u>For the creativity to manifest in the way that you are seeking.</u>

<u>Take a few moments to sensualize this happening . . .</u>
<u>. . . and allow yourself to meditate . . .</u>
<u>. . . and allow the creativity to flow into you . . .</u>
<u>. . . for as long as you wish.</u>

■   ■   ■

When you are ready, close and ground your meditation.

In this chapter, we have worked with adding theta brain waves to your alpha imagery to create a meditation brain-wave pattern of alpha and theta waves that brings depth and breadth to your state of consciousness and meaning and profundity to your content of consciousness in meditation. In order to allow this depth and profundity to manifest in the outside world, we will need to add beta brain waves back to the meditation state.

But first it's important to look at the meaning and experience of delta brain waves. These waves operate at the lowest frequencies, offering us access to the unconscious insight, empathy, intuition, and radar that can be such an important aspect of mastery.

OUR INTUITIVE RADAR

Exploring Delta Brain Waves

D elta waves are the lowest and slowest of our brain-wave frequencies, ranging from 4 down to 0.5 cycles per second. Stop and take a moment to consider how slow this really is, compared to our highest frequency "thinking" beta waves; 0.5 Hz is one emission every 2 seconds compared to 38 emissions per second in high beta. Even theta, our subconscious, is 4 to 8 cycles per second. So delta is below the speed of the subconscious. It is the unconscious.

We produce delta brain waves while we are asleep—while we are literally unconscious. But sometimes we produce delta waves in combination with other waves while we are awake. When this is the case, I like to call delta our "radar."

It is that part of us that reaches out on the most unconscious levels to intuit or understand what is happening. It is that which helps us reach into other people to feel what they are feeling and deeply understand what they are thinking. As such, delta helps provide our intuition, our empathy, our insight.

This inner knowing can range from everyday life experiences to extraordinary psychic phenomena. Delta is present in the brain-wave patterns of healers, regardless of the techniques they are using.

Channelers and those who receive information from other realms as well as those who are in touch with the collective unconscious exhibit high amplitude delta waves. Spiritual masters frequently produce large amounts of delta. But delta can also be experienced uncomfortably as an oversensitivity to external stimuli.

Below, we will look at the variety of delta experiences besides sleep. In order for you to be aware of your delta experience and to make use of any of the unconscious, intuitive, or spiritual content of the delta, you must also have other frequencies present at the same time so that the information can be received by your conscious mind. The awakened mind, with its full complement of beta, alpha, theta, and delta, will give you the greatest conscious access to your delta brain-wave content. But it is also possible to be at least partially aware of the contents of your unconscious mind without alpha and theta fully connecting your delta to your conscious beta.

Examples of Personal Experience of Delta Radar

- You know the phone is going to ring right before it does.

- You think of a friend a few minutes before you "bump into" him or her.

- You feel an unexplained pain, only to find later that your child was hurt at that exact time.

- You know what someone is going to say before they say it.

- You know exactly what someone is feeling, even though they are trying hard to mask it and other people are fooled.

Some people are capable of "talking to each other" with these brain waves without opening their mouths or voicing a sound. A student of a well-known spiritual teacher shared her experience:

"We sat with each other for over an hour. We had a long and intricate conversation in which I asked him many personal questions, and he gave me the answers. It was only when we had finished and I said 'Thank you' that I realized that for the entire time neither one of us had uttered a word!"

BETA AND DELTA IN COMBINATION

Whether or not we receive the information delta has to offer consciously in our beta thinking mind can depend on how much access we have to the frequencies in between beta and delta—alpha and theta. In other words, is the bridge open enough to allow the flow of information from delta all the way up to beta? If we have the combination of beta and delta brain waves with no interconnecting bridge of alpha or theta, then we're "thinking" with one part of our being and "intuiting" with another part of our being. If the beta overrides the delta, we may not even "hear" the information in delta. Or we may hear it but not understand it. Or we may even understand it but not act on it.

Have you ever had a "feeling" that you should do something but you did not understand it and therefore did not act on it? Later, when it turns out that you should have followed your intuition, you might say to yourself, "Why didn't I do that?" or "I knew at the time I should have done that!" And yet often, should the same thing occur again, you still do not act. This is because we're not trained to trust our intuition. And each time we ignore this intuition, we're sending it a message that it doesn't work or is unnecessary. The more you ignore "that feeling" that you are going to knock the glass off the counter if you don't move it, or that you should turn right instead of left to avoid the traffic, and don't act on it, the less this information will come to you. And this is only the mundane and the trivial. This may not seem important, but the next time it might be about slowing your car down to avoid an accident up ahead, or avoiding a relationship with a person who turns out to be a crook. Then it may be absolutely vital that you listen to that intuitive feeling.

If the channels are not fully open between beta and delta, it is still possible to have a very strong intuitive impulse that you act on without really realizing it. One of my students who did this all the time had the reputation for always "landing on his feet," even though he didn't realize or understand why.

But how much more rewarding it is, not to mention useful, to realize that you are experiencing your intuition and allow yourself to follow it. You may never know whether or not you would have actually knocked the glass off the table, but you can rest assured in the fact that you're not going to, because you felt the risk and acted on it by moving the glass. This sends the message to your intuition that you are responding to it and will encourage it to be even stronger and more accurate in the future. I know that the examples I have given are commonplace; however, acting on the mundane exercises the muscle so that it will be ready and in good shape for the important.

Delta with Some Alpha and Theta Bridge

If the frequencies of alpha and theta are open enough so that the conscious is in some way connected to the unconscious, then we'll have a greater understanding that our intuition is telling us something and we need to choose whether or not to act. This then becomes a question of whether or not we wish to listen to our delta. I am not proposing a hierarchy from beta analysis to delta intuition; I'm only proposing that you have absolutely as much information at your fingertips as possible so that you can make an accurate and appropriate choice. Again, this is mastery.

So can delta lead us astray? Of course it can. Just as our thoughts and analyses can ultimately be wrong, so can our intuition. We have just as much need to educate and fine-tune our intuitive skills as we do to educate and fine-tune our analytical skills.

Too Much Unskilled Delta

This can be especially problematic if we have too much delta of the uneducated and unskilled variety. Imagine a situation where you walk into a room full of people and make a beeline for the person who is feeling the worst. Not only do you know who is feeling bad, but also somewhere inside yourself you feel that you ought to fix them. Or, even worse, you start feeling bad yourself for no reason. You can't ascertain the difference between your feelings and the feelings of others. What we have here is a boundary problem.

> Excessive delta can create boundary problems.

In this situation, you have intuited the other person's feelings without knowing it—taking on their negative emotions. It is possible to go through life this way, being buffeted from emotion to emotion, unable to stop being affected over and over again by the strong feelings of others. You may feel excessively responsible for them, wanting to take care of them and make them feel better simply because you really want to make yourself feel better. This susceptibility to the moods, needs, and problems of others can even make it hard to know who you really are.

I had a client who kept moving farther and farther out into the country, farther and farther away from civilization. He felt flooded by thoughts and came to me to learn beta mastery. As he described it to me, he experienced only beta and nothing else. In fact, there were so many "thoughts" running around his head that keeping himself isolated far away from other people was the only way he felt he could still his mind to an acceptable level. He wanted to know how to turn his beta off.

When I questioned him further, he reported that when he was around people, he would worry and feel anxious—"inundated and overwhelmed." In his mind was a tangled mixture of different kinds of "thoughts" that didn't actually make much sense to him, and he just wanted to get away from them.

His brain waves were surprising. In his normal waking state, he had very little beta, some alpha, and quite a bit more theta. But his primary operating frequency was delta. His lack of beta told me that he was not actually "thinking" in the normal sense of the word. The content of his mind was primarily coming from delta. The nature of delta is such that it can act like an antenna of perception, allowing us to sense the emotions, moods, nuances, and mental states of those around us. What he had understood to be his out-of-control beta thought was actually what he was sensing from other people. Once he understood this, he was able to learn to increase his beta and have a greater access to his own thinking abilities, while at the same time decreasing his delta to filter out the thoughts of others.

DELTA AND HYPERVIGILANCE

Boundary issues affect everyone. But the people with the greatest difficulty have what we call **hypervigilance.** The delta of hypervigilance has usually been developed from survival needs, or at least the need for self-protection. Imagine the abused child waiting at home for her parents. Her delta—her radar—is reaching out strongly as an early warning system. Is Mom going to come home drunk? Is Dad going to hit her? Will the day be safe, or is there danger? She developed her delta to help protect herself. But now she is grown up. Her parents are gone. The immediate danger that they presented is gone, but the delta remains. Her hypervigilance is just as strong as ever, but now she is "reading" the minds of other people without even realizing it.

If this ability were trained, she could perhaps become a good psychic. At least she could be an empathetic and understanding person. But she needs to learn how to use her delta appropriately and how to protect herself from the onslaught of others. She also might need to do some inner work on herself to heal the wounds left from her dysfunctional or abusive childhood so that she has the ability to use her potentially valuable delta for her own and others' benefit.

CREATING BOUNDARIES WHILE EXPANDING DELTA

The following meditation is designed to help you explore the boundaries of your intuition and unconscious. As with all aspects of mastery, it is optimum to have choice—choice of where your boundaries are and how strong your delta is.

I have Max Cade to thank for the original idea for this meditation. I found as I took off from his starting place and adapted and expanded it that it provided an excellent learning tool to experience our personal boundaries.

This meditation is best done in a group or in a room with several people in it. If you are trying to do it alone, just imagine the presence of others in the room.

THE BUBBLE

Allow yourself to sit comfortably, and close your eyes.
Take a few moments to center yourself, relax your body, and still
  your mind.

Begin by seeing yourself alone, seated at the center of a large
  bubble,
like a soap bubble.
You can feel the bubble all around you,
enclosing you from the top of your head to the bottom of your feet.
You can almost see it shimmer and glisten.
We could say that this bubble represents your consciousness—
everything that you are aware of at this moment inside and outside
  yourself.

Your consciousness bubble . . .
Your personal space . . .
Feel it around you.
Your consciousness bubble.

Now, picture yourself seated at the center of another bubble, much
    larger this time,
encompassing the size of a large room.
We could say that this bubble represents your subconscious—
everything contained within the depths of your personal being.

Your subconscious bubble . . .
Feel it around you
and just be aware of the experience of this.
Your subconscious bubble.

And now, picture yourself seated at the center of a vastly larger bubble,
the size of a large cathedral or football field.
We could say that this bubble represents your unconscious—
everything that you have ever been aware of
inside and outside yourself,
and you have the capacity for total recall.
Your unconscious.

Now allow yourself to return to the first bubble,
your consciousness bubble.
Feel it around you,
encompassing you from the top of your head to the bottom of your
    feet.
This is your personal space,
your boundaries.
Allow yourself to simply feel this bubble enclosing your
    consciousness,
and just be aware of the experience of this.

And now, very gently allow your bubble to begin to expand,
To encompass another person in the room.

What does it feel like when they pop into your bubble?
When they enter your personal space?
What happens to your boundaries?
Without judgment,
Without analysis,
Just be aware of the feeling of this.

And continue to allow your bubble to grow,
slowly taking in another person in the room . . .
and another . . .
and another . . .

Without judgment . . .
Without analysis . . .
Just be aware of the experience of each person entering your
    bubble.

What happens each time a person enters your bubble?
What kind of response do you have?
Do different people give you different responses?
Again, try to experience this without beta, without analysis, and
    without judgment.

Continue expanding your bubble until everyone in the room
is enclosed in your consciousness bubble . . .
one large group consciousness . . .
and just be aware of the feeling of this.

And now you can begin
to expand your bubble beyond the confines of the room.
Allow your bubble to expand to include someone you love.

And just be aware of the experience of this person entering your
    consciousness bubble,
your personal space,
your boundaries.

And continue to allow your consciousness bubble
to expand,
including as many people as you wish.

Time and distance are irrelevant.
Simply be aware of what it feels like to send your radar outward
to someone you love.

■   ■   ■

And now, in a few moments,
You are going to be ready to
slowly begin to allow your bubble to shrink.
Excluding first one person
and then another,
notice your experience as each person pops out of your bubble . . .
person by person . . .
without judgment
and without thought.

Continue to allow your bubble to shrink,
excluding person after person
until you are back,
alone,
seated at the center of your small bubble,
like a soap bubble
surrounding you from the top of your head to the bottom of your feet.

Just be aware of the feeling of this . . .

Now, take a few moments
To become aware of your experience in this meditation.

What did you learn about yourself?
Were you more comfortable expanded or contracted?
Why?
What were your emotions as you expanded and contracted your
    bubble?
Did you catch yourself analyzing or judging?
What does it tell you about your sense of boundaries?

■   ■   ■

When you are ready, allow your meditation to close,
And return to a normal waking state.

This is a meditation that you can practice at any time in any location. It will help you to understand your sense of boundaries and
your personal space, not to mention your connection and communication with others. I suggest you try a variation of this exercise in
many different situations. For example, if you're in a store and the
clerk is either in a bad mood or not serving correctly, you can use
this exercise either to (a) help understand him or her better and create greater empathy for this individual or (b) create a boundary that
excludes this person and protects you from his or her bad mood.
Experiment with it to see how this exercise can serve you best. Notice how it can fine-tune the experience of your radar.

This is an especially helpful exercise to try with someone you
are having trouble communicating with. This may be anyone—your
spouse, your boss, a colleague, a client, a waiter in a restaurant . . .
Notice what happens to your communication after you have put
them into your consciousness bubble. But again remember: You
can always keep them out if that feels more useful or more comfortable.

A DOCTOR'S EXPERIENCE . . .

One of my students, an M.D. in a group practice who recently learned this meditation, writes, "Just this past Thursday I was arbitrating a very emotional and delicate meeting with our general surgeons. I knew the meeting was going to be tough. . . . As I feared, the meeting became volatile and close to impasse. I still had no answers. I decided to send delta waves around the room and put everyone in a calm, cool and collected bubble. I certainly take no credit for my limited psychic powers, but within short order, some of the most stubborn people on the face of the Earth started compromising and a resolution was achieved."

Accessing and nurturing the abilities of the unconscious mind is a highly valuable experience and a useful skill. Just be sure that you do not develop inordinate sensitivity, by keeping clear boundaries and protecting your personal space.

Delta and Healing

Strong delta brain waves are seen consistently among healers and especially masters practicing the healing arts. I have been involved in all aspects of healing for more than twenty-five years and have had the opportunity to study the brain waves of healers in Europe, North and South America, and Asia in a large variety of situations using many different modalities. Most of the healers produced some form of the awakened mind brain-wave pattern during the act of healing; however, the most consistent similarity among all of the healers was the production of delta waves while practicing their art.

The most consistent similarity among all healers is the production of high-amplitude delta waves.

Why is the unconscious so important to healing? Could it be some form of tapping into the universal or the collective? Could it actually be a measure of some form of energy or *chi* moving through the body? There is much information about delta that we have yet to learn. However, far from the generally accepted idea that delta is produced only in sleep, I see delta as an essential presence during healing activity.

In fact, I have taken some astounding delta measurements on Chi Kung masters doing the healing art of Tui Na. Tui Na is an ancient form of Oriental Chi Kung healing that involves both physical and energetic manipulation. The basis of this practice is the master using his own energy and usually, but not always, his hands to move the *chi* or energy, which runs throughout the body in a circulatory flow in the energy channels called meridians.

The master can use his own energy, usually sent out of his hands or fingers into the body of his student or patient, to affect his or her energy as he sees fit. This is based on the premise that a correct flow or balance of energy exists in the body of a healthy individual, and when that energy is blocked or out of balance, the individual's physical, emotional, mental, or spiritual health (these terms are a Western, not an Eastern, differentiation) is compromised. The master improves the energy flow of his student, thereby improving his or her health.

I have been both the fortunate recipient and the interested observer of Tui Na Chi Kung treatment by a number of Oriental Chi Kung masters and can attest to its power. One such master was Dr. Ni Wen Den of Lukang, Taiwan. Dr. Ni teaches in Taipei at the National Medical Research Academy and is vice president of the China Traditional Chiropractic Association as well as being a well-known and accomplished Chi Kung master.

In a remarkable experience, I actually thought that Dr. Ni had turned on some sort of heating element in the table I was lying on, the heat in my legs was so hot, until I realized that that would be impossible, and it was the energy in my legs heating up due to the blast he was giving me from his hands. After many years of experience of a large variety of energetic healing arts and healers, I was still astonished.

I was so astounded that I convinced him to let me measure his brain waves the next day. The amount of delta that this Chi Kung master produced while practicing his healing was nothing less than remarkable. It was easily ten times the normal amount of delta that a good meditator produces during meditation. At one point, he actually increased his delta production to about fifty times that of normal. I suspect that by this time we may have been measuring more than just his brain waves—that somehow we were measuring his *chi* as well.

While the rest of his brain waves faded in and out of an awakened-mind pattern, depending on what he was doing at the time, his delta remained strong throughout. Dr. Ni defines mastery as, "The heart and the brain come together, and the energy comes out of my hands." He says of meditation, "Meditation and mastery are related. Meditation, as long as it is done correctly, helps the *chi* flow in your body. . . . When *chi* is flowing smoothly, your emotions calm down, reach a state of clarity of mind; then the intuition comes, so when one is facing difficult situations or problems in life, he can react promptly and properly."

Another master with whom I have spent several months in Taipei is Master Wu, a fifth-generation Chi Kung master—his skill was passed down to him from father to son for five generations. He is a humble man with a good heart who "simply wants to help people and feels it is his destiny to do his job." He works with people that the rest of the medical society has rejected as being "too difficult" or "incurable." He considers it his inborn responsibility to "help people who can't get help from other doctors."

Master Wu's delta is so strong that he often does not want his patients to tell him what their problems are, preferring to trust his own intuition rather than to be misled by their [beta] interpretations of what is wrong. All you have to say is, "I hurt," and he will find the source of the pain. He explained to me (through my translator) that he "gets inside someone to feel what is happening." This is a perfect example of the use of his extraordinary delta production. In the particular spinal issue I was dealing with, he was able to touch and alleviate my back pain in a way that no other doctor, healer, or practitioner of any kind has ever been able to do. Indeed, it felt to me like he was "inside" my body. And I owe him a debt of deep gratitude for the healing he was able to do on me.

Delta being present during healing does not depend on any specific healing technique or belief system. Delta is available to, or used by, successful healers everywhere. While the Chi Kung healers are Buddhist and Taoist in their personal spiritual practices, another form of healing is that of the Christian Pentacostal healer. The strongest and most effective Christian healer I have met and had the opportunity to measure is Rev. Robert Crickett, director of Rob Crickett International Ministries and a healing evangelist for Jesus' gospel in the Urantia Papers.

Born in New Zealand and now living in Australia when he is not traveling the world giving healing ministry, Rob has developed an inner relationship with "the Holy Spirit or Holy Mother, Christ, Michael, and Paradise Father." In healing, he calls in whichever combination of these powerful energies is appropriate for the particular issue he is working on and transmits that to his client. His delta amplitude is, as in the other healers mentioned, amazingly strong. People who are healed by him have a direct experience of that energy coming in and feel the presence of God. The results can vary from a shift in stuck thoughts to a bodily experience of improved health and well-being to a great sense of spiritual expansion.

While many healers have a particular devotional spiritual practice, others do not. The main common factor I have observed and experienced in healers all over the world is that they all have some personal connection to an ineffable, universal, expanded consciousness. While the word "God" is appropriate to many, some have other definitions or language for their "source." However, when I intently question people, I realize that they are all referring to the same thing. If you learn all of the languages of "God" or "consciousness" and follow each individual's path back to the source, there is a common meeting ground. And they are all demonstrating that connection with their higher amplitude delta (in combination with an awakened mind, which we will talk about in the next chapter).

Currently one of England's top healers and a close personal friend, Elizabeth St. John is **clairsentient.** While a clairvoyant "sees" what is happening in and for other people and uses that information to help them in some way, Elizabeth "feels" what is happening inside them. Somehow, by adjusting that feeling in herself while "allowing a cosmic energy to travel through that adjustment," she is able to transmit that adjustment as healing to them. She often does not lay on hands or even touch them. Simply by her walking into a hospital room and standing in the doorway, she heals and people get better. Elizabeth's delta is, as in the above healers, an extremely strong component of her awakened mind.

I had my first experience of delta in healing in my early twenties with the late Rose Gladden. She remains one of England's premier healers of all times and was one of the individuals with whom Max Cade did his early original research. I was in the interesting position of watching Rose hooked up to the Mind Mirror as well as being able to see how my own brain waves were affected. Rose's awakened mind was dependable and stable, and her delta, while she was healing, was especially strong. What I was not prepared for, as I had only been involved in studying brain waves for a few years, was how *my* delta was affected by her laying-on-of-hands healing. It expanded to more than ten times my normal (which was not small) and stayed that way for more than an hour after the healing had finished.

An exercise you might enjoy that can help develop the healing aspects of delta and the awakened mind is a practice in the gathering of healing energy for transmission. After you have practiced this meditation, you can give this healing energy to others by simply placing your hands on them, or you can place your hands on yourself and simply allow yourself to receive.

GATHERING THE HEALING ENERGY FOR TRANSMISSION TO OTHERS

Close your eyes and allow your mind to remember your meditation state.
Remember the depth of meditation . . .
What it feels like inside . . .
What your landmarks and keys are . . .
And begin to return to that place now.
Begin to take that depth of meditation into you.
It's almost a sense of moving through different states of consciousness as you go down,
Down and in . . .
Down and in . . .
Down . . . and . . . in . . .

■   ■   ■

As you move deeper into your meditation, you can feel the various tensions in your body letting go . . .
Throughout your body, waves of relaxation and release.
Letting go . . .

Allow any thoughts, images, or outside disturbances to become completely irrelevant
As you move into that deeper state which is within you . . .

Perhaps you find a light there . . .
Or colors . . .
Signposts to help you on your journey . . .
Guidance to take you further . . .

And deeper . . .
To a place that opens inside you.

A place of freedom . . .
A place that knows no bounds . . .
Has no limits . . .
Other than the limits you choose to impose . . .

From within this space now,
you can begin to contact the healing energy that exists in the
    universe.

■ ■ ■

You might sense it as a vibration . . .
As a light . . .
As a sound . . .
Or a voice . . .
As a vision . . .
Or a sensation . . .
Or just a kind of knowing that it is there . . .

And you can begin to take this healing energy into you,
Feeling it running through your body . . .
Through your spirit . . .
Through the very core of your being.

■ ■ ■

If there is any particular area within you that needs healing,
Concentrate the healing energy into that area.
Become aware.
Notice the changes as the energy moves in you . . .
Allow the healing energy to move over you and through you

Like a shower of iridescent flashes of light and sparks.
Allow the exquisite sensation to make its way
To your mind,
To your knowledge,
And allow yourself, if you wish, to have a vision.

■   ■   ■

And again, get in touch with the energy of healing.
Now, as you draw it into your body,
You may become aware of the source of that energy, or you may
    not—
It doesn't matter.
Just know that it comes from a place of wholeness,
A place of universal consciousness,
A place of divinity.

And as you draw it in, bring it down through the top of your head,
Through your heart,
All the way down to the base of your spine
to energize and recharge your vital forces.

And as you take in the energy now,
Bringing it in through the top of your head and down through your
    heart,
Take it also down through your arms,
Coursing down your arms,
And you feel your hands becoming energized.
Feel your arms as channels.
The energy coming in through the top of your head,
through your heart,
and down your arms,
Moving to your hands
And out through the palms of your hands.

■ ■ ■

Let the heart and the brain come together and the energy come out
   of your hands.

■ ■ ■

Sensualize it radiating outward from your palms.
You might feel it as a tingling . . .

Allow yourself to use this energy emanating from your hands for
   healing . . .
in whatever way you wish,
Either by placing your hands on another person
And giving them this universal healing energy . . .
Or by placing your hands on your own body to heal yourself . . .
In whatever way you choose, use this energy to heal,
Taking as long as you wish . . .

■ ■ ■

And in your own time,
And in your own way,
Give your thanks and appreciation for what you have received
And allow yourself to close your meditation
Without shutting off to the source of the healing energy.

■ ■ ■

When you are ready, allow yourself to return.
Reemerge and reawaken,
Arousing yourself and becoming present,
back in the outside space with your eyes open.

THE NEXT STEP

At this point, if you have worked your way consistently through the book, you have learned relaxation, stilling the mind or beta mastery, alpha development, theta development, and delta development. When you put these practices together, you have been developing the ability to meditate. The brain-wave state of meditation is basically alpha, theta, and delta with little or no beta.

The awakened mind state of mastery, however, is beta, alpha, theta, and delta all at the same time. In other words, awakening the mind requires the ability to think and act consciously while maintaining access to the meditation state inside. The easiest and most effective way to train this state is by learning to meditate first without beta, as we have been doing, then adding the appropriate beta back to that meditation state to create an awakened mind.

In the next chapter, we will work with specific ways to add beta to your meditation pattern, to begin to learn to develop the brain-wave pattern of the awakened mind.

THE INTRICATE SYNTHESIS
OF MASTERY

Beta, Alpha, Theta, and Delta,
and the Awakened Mind

Awakening the mind requires not only the ability to access the lower-frequency brain waves found in meditation, but also the ability to produce conscious, aware, attentive thought *at the same time.* This is the brain-wave pattern of simultaneous beta, alpha, theta, and delta called **the awakened mind** that has been found in individuals of extraordinary accomplishment, practicing a myriad of disciplines. From yogis and swamis, to artists and musicians, to CEOs and scientists, we have identified the state of creativity, insight, and all forms of high performance and mastery. This chapter will show you the next and final step in the step-by-step training program for teaching yourself to access this state.

In developing the foundations of mastery, you began in Chapter One by learning the arts of relaxation and stilling the mind to prepare for and assist in producing a meditation brain-wave state. This skill of learning to control, reduce, and eventually eliminate beta thinking is essential in order to be able to truly access the important lower frequencies of alpha, theta, and delta that provide the inner wisdom of mastery. Then you developed the sensualization skills and imagery ability of alpha to open the bridge to the subconscious and give the information that resides in theta a cloak of images to carry it up to your conscious mind. Next, learning to actually meditate gave you entrée to the awareness inherent within these lower frequencies. There, you contacted the subconscious—the storehouse of creativity, the place of spiritual connection, and the opening to the intuition, insight, and inner perceptions of theta. Finally, you explored the unconscious—that intuitive radar that can also give you access to the universal and the collective and even healing energy.

To attain mastery, you now need to add the ability to *think* in beta to the meditation brain waves of alpha, theta, and delta. This will allow you to have tangible expression of your awakening in the outside world. Without the ability to think provided by beta brain waves, our awakening would remain "inactive" and "unmanifest."

So how do we go about the right way of adding the beta or conscious thought back to our now-developed meditation state of consciousness? There are two major approaches to this. But, to help us understand them, first we need to look at the relationship between the state of consciousness and the content of consciousness.

There are two ways of looking at consciousness—*state* of consciousness and *content* of consciousness. The state can be seen in terms of the actual brain-wave pattern, while the content is the thoughts, feeling, emotions . . . the *material* of the mind. We address the state of consciousness by learning to master the specific brain-wave categories.

The content may take several different forms, depending on the brain-wave state in which it is being experienced. When we remove the beta content by quieting our thoughts, we create a clear and empty field for the content of the alpha and theta waves to arise in. This content may include sensory images, daydreams, repressed memories and emotions, simple awareness of whatever is, or inspirational or spiritual insights. When we add useful and appropriate beta brain waves back into the alpha/theta meditation pattern, creating an awakened mind brain-wave pattern, we have fertile ground for such content as creativity, problem solving, and self-healing. The awakened mind brain-wave pattern or *state*, with this kind of valuable, beneficial and constructive *content*, gives us what I call a **high-performance mind**. To be in an awakened-mind state is to be in a state of readiness or potential. To have a high-performance mind, you must know how to *use* your awakened mind correctly.

The essential requirement of the awakened mind brain-wave pattern is that it has an open channel for a *free flow of information between the unconscious, subconscious, and conscious mind.* This flow of information needs to be open in *both* directions, so that we can, for example, understand and manifest our subconscious impulses by bringing them *up* from the subconscious to the conscious mind through this open channel, or we can think about an idea or concept in our conscious mind and send it *down* this open channel from the conscious to the subconscious, where we can seek additional insight.

In other words, the origin of the content may be in either the conscious or the subconscious mind. But once the content is there, it can be experienced, understood, and utilized by all of the brain-wave states. So the deepest hidden unconscious awareness may be made manifest, learned from, and acted upon in conscious ways; and, conscious real-life problems or questions may be solved in or helped by the deeper unconscious and subconscious mind. This is awakening. This is mastery.

"The 'flow' state—when the creative muse is 100% present—is the artist's holy grail; no drink, drug, or flesh can rival the power of God moving through you."

JOSHUA LEEDS, author, producer, composer

So let's return to the two major approaches to adding beta back to the alpha, theta, and delta of meditation. Both of them use content to train state. In the first method, we start by accessing the content from the theta through meditation, then, maintaining the alpha-theta state, we add the beta to develop an awakened mind by bringing the content of the theta up to the conscious thought and working with it. In the second method, we approach it from the opposite point of view by first deciding the content in beta and then adding the alpha, theta, and delta to that content to gain insight to the beta thought and develop an awakened mind. In the end, both methods create an open flow of information between beta, alpha, theta, and delta. What differs is the origin of the content and the process of adding the remaining frequencies to the state in which the content originates.

ADDING THE BETA BACK TO THE
MEDITATION STATE

Let's work with the first method. The basic principle at play here is to first access the content in theta, make it visible, tangible, and re-memberable in alpha, then add the thought of beta to consciously work with that subconscious material, understand it, and even heal or transform it, if appropriate.

Chapter Three gave some specific guidelines for accessing theta brain waves, but they are only designed to access "generic" theta. For example, anything could happen inside the rooms in the House of Doors because we aren't looking for content about a specific issue. What if we want to access specific subconscious material?

There are many different "ways in" to the subconscious. Again, using imagery is perhaps initially one of the most direct and effective tools, simply because the imagery opens the alpha bridge as you go down and allows you a better and more immediate conscious awareness of the content. If we want to access specific material, however, we need to find imagery that can guide us to what we are looking for.

INTENTIONALLY ACCESSING SPECIFIC
SUBCONSCIOUS MATERIAL

A meditation like the House of Doors is easy to convert from the generic to the specific. First, you must decide the general category of material in which you are interested. Try to find one image or word that describes it. For example, instead of the phrase "Why am I having so much difficulty with my job right now?" you might want to have an image of your office or a symbol that represents your job in your mind. If you are interested in exploring your relationship, instead of having "Can I improve my relationship with Jane?" in your mind, just use the mental picture of Jane. Depending upon the subtle nuances of the problem you are experiencing and your optimum access sense, you might prefer the smell of her perfume, the sound of your voices talking together, the texture or the feel of her hair, or simply the image of a heart. You can use any sensory image or combination of images that *represents to you* that which you want to explore. It could even be a word, like "Jane," "communication," "relationship," or "love."

Once you have found a sensory image or word for the material you want to explore, go back to the House of Doors meditation. When you are walking down the corridor passing doors, *intentionally find the door with that symbol or label on it*. Open *that* door and explore what is behind it.

Depending on what you find inside, you may want to bring up the more detailed issues once you are in the room. But you need to take it one step at a time and let the subconscious material take the lead. If you open the door with Jane on it and find an image of yourself inside packing your bag to move out of your shared dwelling, you may want to then sit down with that image and have a dialogue. Ask that image of yourself what he needs to do. For example, does he want to improve the relationship or to leave? If he wants to improve the relationship, ask him what needs to happen for that improvement to take place. Once you have received information about what you would like to have happen or what would be appropriate to happen for a beneficial change, *sensualize that change taking place.*

In other words, you are dialoguing with your subconscious through the help of sensory imagery. **You are adding beta (the dialogue) to the alpha and theta.**

If, on the other hand, you open the "relationship" door and find a wedding in progress, you will obviously have a different dialogue. Let the information from the subconscious take the lead. Do not try to control *how* the information comes to you. Simply allow it to well up from the subconscious, and open the channel so that it can be experienced and dealt with on all levels. In order to follow the principle above for making changes inside, you have to access what is going on inside that you want to change.

It is not uncommon for people to have a lack of theta brain waves because some event or events in their past are painfully lodged deep within the subconscious and the psyche has decided to lock those memories away from conscious knowledge. Alternately, the material may be present in theta, but the individual is not producing enough alpha to bridge the gap between the conscious and the subconscious mind, so the content remains buried. It is possible to watch someone who has subconscious material that wants to remain concealed unknowingly and yet skillfully shift his or her brain waves around so that the material remains hidden and inaccessible to the conscious beta mind.

The decisions about how deep to dig and when to let go and not pursue a particular issue are very personal ones. I would never "force" a client to look at buried material. Yet, when they are really keen on accessing it, and when it is getting in the way of their continued emotional and spiritual development, I will definitely help them work through whatever is concealed to a place of satisfactory resolution, if they so desire. And that place differs with each person. Again, if you feel unable to deal with your subconscious content on your own, I strongly suggest you enlist the support of a professional. Signals to watch out for are feeling overwhelmed, afraid, depressed, or having any negative emotion connected with your endeavors that will not go away or threatens your stability in some way. Most people, however, can feel confident and safe in pursuing an exploration of suppressed content through meditation and brain-wave mastery.

The best way to add beta to your meditation pattern is through words—thinking, talking, writing—anything that adds conceptual articulation. But the words must be focused on the material at hand, not just an excuse to wander with your mind.

First let's redo the House of Doors so that it no longer accesses only generic subconscious material but also accesses specific theta and begins to add beta to the meditation pattern. In other words, let's turn the House of Doors from a theta meditation to an awakened-mind meditation. Much of it will stay the same, but notice the underlined key changes.

HOUSE OF DOORS II

Let your mind clear, and focus on your breathing.
(Please spend at least five to ten minutes relaxing before continuing. You may wish to refer back to the foundations of relaxing the body and stilling the mind in Chapter One as preparation for this meditation.)

And now, from this place of deep relaxation and peace,
In your mind, create an environment.
Imagine or create an environment outdoors, somewhere pleasant
   for you.
It could be the mountains, the country, the beach . . .
See it clearly.

Walk around it in your mind.

Using as many senses as possible, explore this environment
carefully.

Experience the colors, the shapes, the textures, the sounds, the
smells.

What is the time of day, the atmosphere, the temperature?

Feel them with your mind.

Make any changes that you would like to make in this environment
to make it safe and secure for you.

■   ■   ■

Now, within this environment, place a house.

Don't go inside yet; just see it from the outside.

You're going to go on a journey through this house.

So, going in through the front door . . .

And passing through an entrance hallway . . .

You find yourself in a room covered in mirrors.

Mirrors all around you.

You notice your image, your reflection, in these mirrors.

Now, passing through the room of mirrors,

You find yourself in a long hallway.

A seemingly endless corridor with rows of doors on either side.

And each of the doors is a different color.

You walk down this hallway, passing door . . . after door . . . after
door . . .

Until you find a door labeled "challenge."

Notice whether this door is on the left or the right,

And notice the color or symbols on the door.

When you are ready, open this door and go into the room that is
behind it.

Take all of the time that you need to very thoroughly explore this
room and its contents.

■　■　■

While you are in this room,
allow yourself to think about what you find here.
Using your beta,
you can dialogue with any other individuals or even objects that are
    present.
You also have the power to make any changes that you want.
Think about what you would like these changes to be,
and allow yourself to sensualize them taking place.

■　■　■

In a few moments, you are going to leave this room.
So allow yourself to take the time now to complete anything that
    you are doing here.
You can always return whenever you wish
if you would like to spend more time here.

And now, when you are ready, leave this room behind
and go back out into the corridor.
Close the door behind you, but don't lock it, so that you can return
    if you wish.
And continue your way on down the hallway,
again passing door after door.

Notice any other doors that you especially want to enter.
If there is another aspect of the "challenge" that you feel drawn to
    explore,
find the door with the appropriate label and allow yourself to
    explore that room.
Is there, perhaps, a room on the opposite side of the hallway
that will give you information or insight?

Once you have located a room to enter,
allow yourself to explore it thoroughly and think about the meaning
  or impact it has for you.

■ ■ ■

Remember that you have the power to make any changes at all that
  you want to make within this room.

■ ■ ■

Now, when you are ready,
begin to complete what you are doing in this room.
Remember that you can always return here if you wish.

And now, leave this room behind.
Go back out into the corridor,
close the door behind you, but don't lock it.

And continue your journey on down the hallway.

Way in the distance, . . .
way down the corridor in front of you . . .
you begin to see the end of the hallway.
The hallway ends at a door marked "solution."
Make your way down the corridor
until you get to the "solution door" and,
after noticing any color or images on the door,
open this door and explore what is behind it.

Take all the time that you need to very thoroughly explore this space.

■ ■ ■

When you are ready,
allow yourself to sit down in this space
and think about the experience you have had in this room.
Using beta, think about what the solution might mean to you
and how you can apply this to your life.

■   ■   ■

When you have spent as much time as you need exploring
    "solution,"
allow yourself to come to completion for now,
and prepare to leave this space.

When you're ready,
go back out into the corridor
and close the door behind you.
Remember not to lock it, so you can return whenever you wish.

And this time, retrace your steps back down the hallway the way
    you came.
Back past any other doors that you entered.
Back into the room of mirrors.
Notice any changes in your reflection, your image.
Back through the entrance hallway.
Back out the front door.
Back into your environment.
Making any changes that you want to make within your environment,
find a comfortable place to sit . . .
and to meditate.
Meditate on what you experienced in the House of Doors.
And what it might mean to you.

Think about how this experience relates to your life,
and how you can integrate it and use it in the future.

■ ■ ■

When you are ready,
Find a few "keys" to bring back with you when you reawaken,
To remind you of where you have been,
what you have experienced,
and what you have gained from that experience.
These keys may be images, symbols, body sensations, colors,
    emotions, words, or phrases . . .
anything that will help you remember your experience . . .
even tastes, smells, sounds, and textures that were present in your
    meditation.

■ ■ ■

In your own time, when you are ready,
begin to allow yourself to find a closure for your meditation.
In your own time, when you are ready,
begin to allow yourself to return.
Back to the outside space.
Allow yourself to reawaken and return
Feeling alert . . . and refreshed.

Take several deep, rapid breaths,
And allow yourself to stretch, beginning with fingers and toes.
Open your eyes and reenter the outside space.

In the previous House of Doors meditation, we added the beta and thought about the content *at the end of the meditation.* This still facilitates the flow of information from the subconscious to the conscious mind, but it is more of a *sequential* flow—meditate first, then add beta thought to bring the information up. In this second version, we add the beta right there in the middle of the meditation *while we are still meditating.* This helps facilitate the *simultaneous* production of beta, alpha, theta, and delta, awakening the mind.

Using the concepts of "challenge" and "solution" is still generic—enough to provide a broad category that will work for just about anybody in any situation. Please feel free to personalize this meditation even more by adding your own specific challenge.

The following examples of people's experiences within the rooms of this meditation illustrate the diversity and variations that can occur.

Susan, a therapist of long standing, had been working on the issues of scarcity and having abundance in her life. Her challenge room contained the Dalai Lama, who told her, "Luxury is an inner state." She realized for the first time that she was actually entitled to luxury. Her solution room contained Moses holding an upside down version of the Ten Commandments. She was startled to read them in the positive rather than the negative: "Thou shalt have love. Thou shalt enjoy your life. Thou shalt have things come easily . . ." In her emotion-filled account following the meditation, she acknowledged, "This feels life-changing."

Tony, a high-tech businessman, saw a dark staircase going down into the depths of infinity in his challenge room. The door was labeled "life's purpose." He did not know what to make of it and did not understand how to discover his life's purpose until he got to the solution room. Here he received a ray of light through his heart. As he left through the room of mirrors, he saw himself as a peaceful and wise old man in a white robe with long, silver hair. He said, "I walked away a different person than when I walked in. My life's purpose is in my heart."

Marirose, a law student turned divinity student, described her challenge room as containing a dour old woman who, with a surly tone of voice, said, "What do you think you're doing? You can't do that!" She knew that it was about moving from law school to divinity school. In her solution room, she "was filled with light and peace that swept through every cell of my body." She came away with a feeling of "rootedness, peace, joy, and dance."

The following meditation uses the basic principles of accessing alpha through imagery, accessing theta through specific content that needs healing, and then adding beta back through words—which I call "subconscious dialogue."

Personal Transformation Meditation

(I have presented this meditation in steps or stages. The initial instruction of each stage is <u>underlined</u>, followed by further explanation.)

<u>Be aware of the issue or problem that needs transformation.</u>

Consider what it is that you want to change, transform, or heal. Put that in the back of your mind and leave it there. Then allow your mind to clear.

Be aware that later, when you are in the depths of meditation, you may find that another issue, totally different from the one you thought you wanted to work on, emerges from your subconscious. In this exercise, allow yourself to be open to working on whatever appears to you to have the most need and easiest access for transformation. Certainly be open to working on an issue you had not "thought" of working on.

The reason we think about it first and put that concept in the back of the mind to draw out later is so that we won't have to resort to beta for the origin of the impulse later in the meditation. We want this concept, even though we have first identified it in beta, to originate in theta.

If you want to be absolutely sure that the concept originates in theta and has little or no beta impulse, you can always use generic concepts like working on "whatever is getting in the way of my growth and evolution."

Still your mind and relax your body
(reduce or eliminate initial beta).

Remember what it feels like to be in your state of meditation and allow yourself to return there.

Focus on your breathing, and gently let yourself breathe easily and deeply, using your hand as a lever to slow your breathing down for a minute or two if you wish.

Remember to relax your tongue. If you feel any pulling on the back of your tongue, it means that you are talking to yourself. If you relax your tongue completely, you can't talk to yourself, and it will be much more difficult to think. Anytime an unwanted thought comes through, relax your tongue as you exhale and breathe the thought away. Breathe relaxation into your mind when you inhale, and breathe away thoughts when you exhale . . .

Relax your body (continue beta mastery and preparation for
alpha and theta).

Check to make sure that the whole of your body is relaxed.

Gently scan your body to make sure you are not holding tension anywhere. Shine a light through it. Notice any areas that are darker than others. Breathe relaxation into those parts of you when you inhale, and breathe away the tension when you exhale. Continue relaxing your body until you can see the light throughout.

Create a healing environment
(using sensory imagery to access alpha).

In your mind, create an environment that is comfortable and healing for you.

It can be indoors or outdoors. Walk around in this environment. Notice the colors . . . the shapes . . . the forms. Be aware of the textures, the atmosphere, the temperature . . . the sounds, the smells, even the tastes. Explore this environment using all of your senses. Make any changes that you want to make, adding anything that you might need for your health and well-being. Create a space that is secure, serene, and safe.

Meditate (continued development of alpha and increased development of theta).
Find a comfortable place within this environment to sit down, and allow yourself to go into a very deep meditation.

Experience a sense of falling . . . falling deeply into relaxation, into warmth . . . into yourself.

Find the part that needs healing (using content to access theta).
From this place of depth inside yourself, you can begin to get in touch with the part of yourself that needs healing, transformation, or change. It may be the issue that you originally thought about before the meditation began, or you may find that a deeper or more meaningful issue comes forward, ready to be healed.

Find some way to allow this part to manifest for you (using alpha imagery to open the channel to the subconscious).
It could be through a symbol, an image, a body sensation, a feeling, a sound, or even a voice in your head. Or it could simply be a sense of knowing that the part is present.

Begin to dialogue (add beta to the alpha and theta).
Ask if it is willing to communicate with you. If it is uncertain, ask what needs to happen to make it more willing.

What follows is a series of questions that you might like to ask this part of you. Each meditation and healing experience is different, so only use these as a guide. You may add, delete, or adapt in any way that is helpful for your process.

How is this part feeling? If it is feeling at all threatened by this experience, you might like to reassure it that what you are in the process of

*doing is for the benefit of your being as a whole . . . that you are doing
this to heal and to help.*

How long has it been there? Is this a new issue or a very old one?

This may lead you to ask, how did it get there?

What does it need or want from you?

What role or purpose does it play in your life?

*What needs to happen for the transformation that you are seeking to
occur?*

*Is this part willing to let this change occur? (If not, what needs to
happen to allow it to become willing?)*

Sensualize. Use as many of your senses as possible to imagine the change taking place.

*Look into the future. Sensualize yourself in the future after this trans-
formation has already taken place.*

*Experience what it looks like . . . what it feels like . . . what it
sounds like . . . even what it smells and tastes like . . . for this part to be
transformed or healed in the way that you want it to be—in the way that
you know that it can be. Use as many of your senses as possible.*

Live the experience.

Give your appreciation.

*Acknowledge that part for all of the hard work that it has done for you.
Even if it has fulfilled a function that you disagree with now, offer your
appreciation for the fact that inside yourself, this part of you thought
that it was working for your benefit.*

*Allow the part to respond to you. Ask it if there is anything else that
it wants to say to you.*

Check to see if any other issues have been stimulated.

*Are there any other parts inside you that want to say something to you?
This inner change may have stimulated other aspects of yourself that are
happy, sad, frightened, disturbed, or pleased with the transformation.
Give them an opportunity to communicate with you.*

If necessary, begin your dialogue again with the new part that seems disturbed. Follow it through to completion.

Allow yourself to begin to find a closure.

When you are ready to complete your meditation, spend a few minutes inside preparing to close, giving your appreciation to your inner parts for their willingness to participate in your healing. You may wish to make an inner agreement to check back inside yourself at some future time to continue this process or to allow yourself further opportunity to meditate. A closure is not necessarily an ending.

Bring the flow up to beta.

Crystallize your experience in a few key images, words, or phrases. Bring those out with you when you awaken from your meditation.

As always, verbalizing, talking into a tape recorder, telling a friend, or writing down what happened will fix the experience firmly in your conscious beta mind so that it will remain present for you and not slip back into your subconscious.

Make sure that you stretch, breathe deeply, and arouse properly before you leave your meditation space.

WORKING WITH CONTENT

You may find that you have accessed material that you are familiar with, and your subconscious dialogues have served to clarify and reinforce inner needs or potential transformation. Or perhaps you have illuminated areas as yet unencountered by your conscious mind. In either case, one meditation session in which you open the channels, allow the flow of information to occur, and use your awakened mind in a high-performance way may not be enough to deal with or complete the particular content with which you are working. You may wish to go back to the same material again and again as you gently foster and encourage the appropriate inner changes.

In these cases, the origin of the material is no longer necessarily in theta. You are now working contiguously with the contents of beta, alpha, theta, and delta, each part offering its own contribution to the understanding and progress of the situation. Let's look at what form those contributions are likely to take within each category of brain wave.

Beta provides the conceptual framework and the descriptive words that define and render precise intellectual delineation of the situation. **Alpha** provides sensory input and illustrates the content through imagery and sensualization. It also links the conscious mind to the subconscious. **Theta** provides the subconscious, inner information or wisdom. In its pure form, this is not experienced with clear imagery, rather having the hazy, dream-like qualities of deep internal reverie. When alpha and theta are experienced together, the theta provides the depth and profundity of the material and the alpha provides the clarity and lucidity of vivid imagery. **Delta** provides the unconscious instinctual and intuitive input, which can be seen as access to the universal mind, or the collective.

Each category of brain wave has its own contribution and part to play in the totality of the awakened mind experience. Each is necessary, and none is more important than the others. They must all work in concert to promote high performance, true mental clarity, and emotional and spiritual awakening. But they don't necessarily all have to work simultaneously to begin to be effective. It is possible for each brain-wave category to play its proper and effective role *almost* independently, one approaching the content fully through its appropriate modality and then, in essence, passing the material along to the next category to be dealt with in its way. Here, the flow of information moves sequentially from the conscious to the unconscious mind and back.

The following meditation applies this principle of the passing of information through the different categories of brain waves to maximize the effectiveness of each modality and ultimately integrate into a single whole through the flow of information. To begin this meditation, *choose content from beta*. Initially, this would ideally be a creative issue or project that you are working on. Perhaps you've come to a standstill or are experiencing a problem of some sort. Or perhaps you simply would like more readily available input as to the way forward in a particular endeavor or enterprise.

WHY THE NAME "EXERCISE YO' GAME"

This meditation is named after a rap song, "Exercise Yo' Game" by the singer/songwriter Coolio, recorded on the Tommy Boy label. I spent a week working at Tommy Boy in New York City, and it turned out to be one of the most creative and interesting "corporate" experiences I have had. The brain waves were fascinating and the awakened minds were many. While there, they gave me several rap albums—ostensibly for my then thirteen-year-old son, John.

When John and I drove to Esalen the next month, we listened to rap for hours on end in the car. One of our favorite songs was "Exercise Yo' Game" on the album *Gangsta's Paradise*. Over and over again I listened to those words till they must have gotten into my subconscious.

Contrary to many rap songs, this one has a very positive theme about doing what it takes to make life work—but from a "street" point of view: "let me show you how to do for self [sic], 'cause ain't nobody gonna do it for you. . . . you got to put yourself in heaven on earth before you pass . . . Have heart; have money. . . . I exercise my game until I have my game perfected." It spoke words applicable to anyone trying to awaken and have a high-performance mind—I really agreed with it!

As a result, during my workshop at Esalen Institute, I created a new meditation practice that came out of the essence of that song and the work I did at Tommy Boy. It has to do with *exercising* the pathway from beta down through alpha then theta to delta and back up again quickly over and over many times in the same meditation, and stopping to write, draw, or create after each cycle. I loved it and so did the group! So I asked Tom

Silverman, founder of Tommy Boy Records, and Coolio for permission to use their title.

Tom Silverman himself has a remarkable awakened mind with very strong theta and delta. His creative accomplishments are apparent, in his music, in his diversity, and in the success of his recording company. I was intrigued by Tom's more-or-less continuous awakened mind brain-wave pattern, so I asked him to comment on creativity . . .

"Listening and looking for signposts that I would normally miss and trusting my intuition works more times than research, control, and force do . . . allowing any possibility and being open to guidance." Wise words indeed.

Remember, to exercise the **flow of information,** you don't have to have it all at once to start using it.

When you practice this meditation, have paper and pen, pencil, or colored drawing implements handy. Practice in an area where you can meditate, write or draw, and return to meditation easily.

EXERCISE YO' GAME

Begin by sitting with your eyes closed and simply *thinking* about that which you wish to work on. Put the creative concept or project into beta by defining it in words.

Next, take the creative concept or project down into alpha by sensualizing it. Don't try to solve any problems; in fact, actively avoid trying to do anything. Simply use your sensory imagery to explore the situation. If you can visualize, *see* the project. Walk around it and view it from all angles. Also allow yourself to *hear* it, *feel* it, even *taste* and *smell* it if you can.

Now comes the tricky part. You have to drop down into theta, taking the creative project into your subconscious, to allow your inner insight and "higher self" to give its input. In order to do this, allow yourself to already be sitting in a relaxing meditation position. Use your landmarks of theta and your theta development techniques to stimulate access to this state. You may want to experience yourself going down a well, or dropping down a long tunnel, or just simply going deeply inside. (If you have trouble with this, return to Chapter Three.)

Plant the seed of the creative endeavor in your subconscious. Remember, you have just been visualizing it, so it's only a short drop to take it further down into the deep. Leave it there for a few minutes to germinate.

Next comes the final essential step of letting go. When you take the project even further down into delta, you literally release it to the unconscious. It's as if you are turning it over to your higher power or figure of divinity or spiritual source. What is necessary here is *true detachment and surrender*. You simply *let it go*.

By giving your creative endeavor to delta, you are asking the powers that be for guidance and assistance. You are letting go of control. Most important, you are letting go of the stranglehold that beta can put on creativity and opening up to the universal and the collective for new, deeper, and broader forms of input and intuitive insight.

Sit in this space for as long as seems suitable—from a few seconds to several minutes. As you enter into this deep and silent space, feel free to ask that you be given the correct images and words when appropriate.

■　■　■

So far, this has been opening up the channels for the flow of information to go *down*. Now it is time to bring the information back up again in reverse order.

Moving from the unconscious delta back up to the subconscious theta, feel a reconnection with *your own* inner insight and wisdom. Feel the stirrings in your subconscious as you bring the project or creative endeavor closer to the conscious border. You may start to sense hazy images tinged in deep blues and purples or start to experience a "sense of knowing" that the information is there.

Now begin to allow alpha images to *form around it*. See, hear, taste, smell, touch, feel the insight. Begin to have concrete images of the solution, or next steps of your creative endeavor.

Now, begin to hear the words connected with those images. Bringing it all the way up to beta, begin to allow words of definition or description to form around the images. Take it all the way up to concrete concepts and thoughts.

When you are ready, open your eyes and write or draw your experience. Ground it in beta by putting it on paper. In effect, you are draining all of the information in your lower frequencies *upward* into your conscious mind. Get it all out as fast as you can. Put it in words. Put it on paper. Fix it in beta.

■ ■ ■

When you are finished you will know it. When the rush of information is over or the "brain dump" is done, stop. Don't force it or labor it.

Now repeat the process. Dip back down again, from beta through alpha to theta to delta, rest there for as long as you need, then bring more information, insight, and inspiration back up again to manifest in your beta reality. Open your eyes and write again.

■ ■ ■

You can continue these cycles many times until the information is flowing freely on its own and you no longer need to distinguish between the different stages, until the flow of information between beta, alpha, theta, and delta is open and free-flowing, until you are comfortable operating in an awakened mind brain-wave pattern and learn to use your high-performance mind.

Now that you have gained an understanding of and are beginning to develop mastery of beta, alpha, theta, and delta, in the next chapters of this book, we will look at applying this mastery to other aspects of your life, from the customary and commonplace to the transformative and numinous.

SELF-EXPLORATION AND UNDERSTANDING

Making the Subconscious Conscious

Awakening the mind intrinsically means the development of a deep, clear, and meaningful understanding of one's internal self—from our own broad spectrum of greater needs and life expectations to our personal internal quirks and idiosyncrasies. Ultimately, mastery means both the self-control and self-expression of these personality traits.

Awakening is about your very carriage in the world—from the greater fulfillment of your life's purpose to the smaller but important personality presentation as you move through your daily life. When you have achieved mastery, both of these fall within your means of understanding and direction.

I am not by any means suggesting that you could or should have some sort of absolute power over your personal ability to manifest— or to always be able to produce tangible expression of your creativity on demand. On the contrary, I believe strongly in the Tao and destiny. Sometimes, being in the right place at the right time is an essential component of our creative flow. Sometimes, it is appropriate to turn our creative endeavors over to our higher power or God, and just wait to see what happens. However, to the greater extent that you can develop an increasingly deeper understanding of your own internal process, you can develop a greater influence on both your internal way of being and your external self-expression of that inner being.

In short, the more you can get to know yourself inside, the more you can have some conscious influence over who you are and how you live your life. This gives you *choice*, which in turn leads to mastery.

CHOICE

I cannot overemphasize the importance of the power of the ability to choose. You can have choice not only of the external, such as choice of where you live, choice of your friends, choice of your career or job, choice of what you read or study, choice of what you eat, choice of how you dress, choice of where you go and how you spend your time. You can also have choice of your thoughts or the contents of your mind, choice of your emotions, choice of your attitudes, choice of your habits, choice of your behavior, choice of your actions, and, very important, choice of your reactions.

As a frequent practitioner of the philosophy of Taoism, I believe strongly in the importance and the power of choice. However, this is not a duality. Perhaps the most important choice of all that you have is the choice to follow your own Tao. This means that you actually have the ability to choose to fulfill your own destiny, your own higher purpose. You have the choice to find your life's work. **You have the choice to develop mastery.**

If we look at this even more closely, we can see that choosing to cultivate mastery means learning to be able to choose our states of consciousness. And through practice, you can do just that.

Although the choice of many masters is to spend much of their time in the brain-wave combination of beta, alpha, theta, and delta— the awakened mind—there are endless variations of that combination, subtleties and nuances shaped by intentions, needs, and personal choices that underlie or determine their state of consciousness at any given time.

I measured the brain waves of Master Lee Fung Shan while he was doing eleven different activities or practices. I have rarely seen so many varieties of the awakened mind on one individual. His combinations of beta, alpha, theta, and delta changed according to his need and intention. He produced the most classic form of the awakened mind while practicing his own personal meditation, the still and peaceful Quan Yin Tsi Tsai meditation, about which he said, "The key is between the exhale and the inhale."

Master Lee is well-known for many abilities, including his power to sprout peanuts and kill bacteria with his mind. On the Mind Mirror, his patterns were remarkably similar during both of those activities. He said that he simply *chose* between whether he wanted to "defeat or to heal." This is a supreme example of choice.

So how do you develop the capacity for choice? You can only acquire *conscious* influence over who you are and how you live your life by getting to know yourself inside.

> Through self-exploration and self-understanding, you can begin to develop the ability to have conscious control of your internal states. This, in turn, leads to choice. And through the choice to be in higher states of conciousness, you can gain mastery.

So how can we get to know and understand ourselves inside? To answer that question, let's go back to the language of brain waves that we have developed so far.

Most of us live our day-to-day lives skimming the surface of our innermost beings, rattling around in our beta waves as we jump from thought to thought. Our times of creativity, when we have them, are often externally linked or content-specific. In other words, creativity may only flow in relationship to an outside project or need. If we are lucky or inventively developed in that arena, then we have access to an aspect of mastery that allows creativity to flow in relationship to that specific content. We may then experience the combination of beta, alpha, theta, and delta that gives us an awakened mind.

The first half of this book showed you how you can develop the awakened-mind state independently of a specific content so that it can be used and experienced in any and all arenas of your life. Now we want to talk about how to use that state for our own self-exploration and understanding—in other words, working with specific rather than generic content. This in turn will feed back into the development of your personal mastery, increasing your inner self-control, abilities, and choice.

> We can use our higher "state of consciousness" to understand and develop personal "content of consciousness." As we continue to work with our internal content, we continue to develop and improve our internal state. As this cycle repeats, we increase our mastery.

So again, we do not want to look for the understanding of our innermost beings in our beta waves. This depth of understanding and profundity can be attained through theta brain waves. But it can only be accessed through the gateway of alpha—the bridge between the conscious and the subconscious mind. We need to reach down to the very depths of ourselves to find both our strengths and our weaknesses and to develop our mastery.

Let's begin this self-exploration by returning to an alpha exercise from Chapter Two (page 70). The Animal Sensualization is a simple "beingness" meditation that helps you to develop alpha brain waves. But having opened this alpha gateway to the subconscious, we can begin to access and add theta to our state to both develop our state of mastery and increase our self-understanding, ultimately giving us the power to make meaningful, permanent internal shifts.

So let's now revisit this beingness meditation and expand it, letting it take us deeper into theta, intentionally giving us a greater knowledge of our own internal strengths, weaknesses, and needs.

ANIMAL SENSUALIZATION II

Sensualize yourself as some kind of animal.

It could be a real animal or a fantasy animal.

If you have trouble identifying what you are, look down at your feet.

What kind of feet . . . or hooves . . . or claws . . . do you have?

What is your skin covering?

How big are you?

What is your shape?

How do you move?

What do you eat?

Where do you live?

What kind of sound do you make?

How do you communicate?

Do you live alone . . . with a mate . . . with a group?

What makes you happy . . . ?

    sad . . . ?

    afraid . . . ?

    strong and powerful . . . ?

What gives you courage?

Live the experience of being this animal for a few minutes.

Sensualize it using as many senses as possible.

(The following deeper investigation will begin to stimulate theta brain waves to add to your alpha.)

Soon you are going to slowly turn back to your human form.
But before you do, take a few moments to focus on the qualities and
  characteristics of your animal form that you would like to bring
  back with you into your human form.

Allow yourself to crystallize these qualities and characteristics into
  two or three things you would like to have with you.

What are the qualities and characteristics you would like to leave
  with your animal?

Leaving your animal form behind now,
meditate on having these qualities and characteristics in your life . . .

Sensualize yourself as you are as a *human* being
with these things fully manifest within you.
Use as many senses as possible and live the experience.

Before you draw your meditation to a close,
  see yourself in the future
with these things as completely integrated aspects of your human
  being.

When you emerge from your meditation,
take several deep, rapid breaths, and allow yourself to stretch and
  open your eyes,
feeling fully alert and awake.

Bring your experience fully to beta by putting into words those
  qualities and characteristics that you discovered in your animal
  being.
Consider for a few minutes how you relate to these things. They are
  probably qualities that you have had all along or that are deeply

meaningful to you. Perhaps you fully manifest them already, or perhaps they have been hidden or not fully fulfilled so far in your life.

This meditation can help you get in touch with those deeper resources and begin to accept them and own them as part of you.

OWNING YOUR INNER CHARACTERISTICS

When I use this type of meditation in seminars, there is a closing process that I often take the meditators through. This involves verbalizing these crystallized positive characteristics to the group in the format of, "My name is _____. I am _____, _____, and _____." It is stated in the affirmative present tense, which allows the meditator to really own in beta that which was uncovered in theta, therefore grounding it in conscious reality.

The difficulty that people sometimes encounter in making such absolute, definitive, and positive statements about themselves is a testament to its importance. They often feel strengthened and empowered by this final round of sharing in a way that simply discussing their experience of the meditation cannot provide.

I would like to suggest that you either speak out loud or write down (preferably both) the characteristics that you identified in this same format. It is very important that you own or embody the qualities. Feel the difference between saying "I am Steve. *In this meditation, I was* strong, powerful, and swift." versus "I am Steve. I *feel* strong, powerful, and swift." versus "I am Steve. I *am* strong, powerful, and swift." Say it out loud using your own name and qualities, and experience the increased power of saying "am" rather than "was" or "feel." This is much more immediate and powerful, ensuring that you *own* your qualities rather than just talk about them.

I have found that endless varieties of animals appear for people in these meditations. Following are examples of four people's experiences.

Anthony was an eagle. His qualities were "far-seeing, vision, freedom, grace of movement, and soaring high." He really appreciated pulling these buried qualities out of his subconscious because in his work (software design) and life, he often found himself lost in intricate detail. He had forgotten how to look at the big picture and felt confined and stuck. Getting in touch with his "inner eagle" allowed him to reconnect with his innate ability to fly high, fulfill his need for long-range planning, and have a better sense of freedom from "the daily drudgery of life."

It is quite possible for two people to have the same animal with completely different qualities and characteristics. Steve was a bear, "fearless, strong, and grounded," connecting with his masculine power. Kate was also a bear, "nurturing, protective, and loving," a mother bear caring for her young. The same animal expressed one person's bold and courageous power while embodying another's maternal love.

The animals don't necessarily need to be real. Sarah was "a dragon who didn't know where its tail was." She was the last of her species and had developed many friendships with other kinds of animals. Her strengths were fire, passion, aliveness, and compassion. From her meditation, Sarah learned, "Big energy creates wakes. I need to be more conscious of how my energy is affecting people around me."

In creating beingness meditations, you don't need to limit yourself to being an animal. You can sensualize and explore your relationship to *anything* in this way, thereby learning about deeper or hidden aspects of your innermost being. For example, you can do a similar meditation in the same way, substituting the following:

PLANT/TREE SENSUALIZATION

Sensualize yourself as some kind of plant or tree.
How big are you?
Where are you growing?

Are you indoors or outdoors?
What kind of soil are you in?
Is it dry . . . or moist?
Fertile . . . or barren?

What kind of roots do you have?
How deep do your roots grow?
How broad do they spread?

Are there other plants growing near you?
How many and what kind?

What color are you?
Do you bear flowers or fruit?

As this plant, what makes you strong?
. . . healthy?
. . . happy?

Live the experience of this plant for a few moments . . .

■　■　■

Soon you are going to slowly turn back to your human form.
But before you do, take a few moments to focus on the qualities and
    characteristics of your plant form
that you would like to bring back with you into your human
    form.

Allow yourself to crystallize these qualities and characteristics
into two or three things you would like to keep with you.

What are the qualities and characteristics you would like to leave
    with your plant?

■　■　■

What do you need as this plant to make your life stronger, healthier,
　happier?

■　■　■

Now sensualize your human being.
Do you have these or similar needs also in your human form?
What needs to take place in your human life
to give you the changes that will make your life stronger . . .
　healthier . . . happier?

Imagine these changes taking place in your life,
using as many senses as possible.

■　■　■

Before you draw your meditation to a close,
see yourself in the future
with these things as manifest in your life.

■　■　■

In your own time,
begin to allow yourself to find a closure for your meditation.

■　■　■

When you emerge from your meditation, take several deep, rapid
　breaths,
and allow yourself to stretch and open your eyes,
feeling fully alert and awake.

■　■　■

*At the close of your meditation, take a few minutes to look at the discoveries you can make about yourself by studying the relationship of your **plant** characteristics and needs to your **human** characteristics and needs.*

For example, if your plant's soil is dry and cracked, not giving you the life-producing nutrients you need, do you also need to find a way to nourish and nurture yourself in real life? Or perhaps if your plant is in a pot that is too small for its roots, what does this tell you about your human environment? If your plant desperately needs more sun, what does that mean to you?

What are the positive qualities and characteristics of your plant form that you want to bring with you to your human form?

Following the same format that I described earlier, you can write or say, "My name is _____. I am _____, _____, and _____."

You can even see what the relationship of your plant is to your animal. What are their similarities? Differences? What can you learn about yourself from looking at all three—plant, animal, and human—characteristics of yourself?

You can play with these beingness meditations in any form you choose. Try writing your own. You can go from the mundane to the outrageous and still learn interesting insights about yourself. For example, imagine you are some kind of *bookshelf*. Are you antique or new? How big are you? Where are you located? What kind of books do you contain?

Or, imagine you are some kind of *book*. Among other questions, "What is written in you?" and "Who reads you?" should give you plenty of food for thought.

Or, on a more enchanting note, imagine you are some kind of *magic potion*. What are you used for? Who uses you? What powers do you have? What can you learn here about your hidden resources and inner desires and abilities.

When we look into the subconscious, we begin to get to know the deep, often hidden parts of ourselves that contain our innermost resources, insights, wounds, blockages, creative inspirations, healing powers, and spiritual wisdom—parts of ourselves that are essential to recognize and own in a conscious way in order to have true mastery.

To begin to understand these individual aspects of ourselves in detail, it is valuable to first have an understanding of the big picture, the whole as opposed to the part. An understanding of where you are in the big picture of your life might sound easy from a beta point of view. You might think, "I want to get married and raise children, have a three-bedroom house in the city, a vacation cottage in the country, earn X amount of money, and be able to retire by the time I'm sixty." Or, "I want to be made a vice president of my company," or "I want to travel around the world."

These are all, in themselves, admirable, worthy, and possibly obtainable goals. But they are all material in nature. What I mean by an understanding of the big picture involves beginning to understand where you are on your own evolutionary path. Our mental, emotional, and spiritual evolution is not covered in the classroom agendas of our childhood education.

Mastery means taking charge of our emotional maturity, self-understanding and, in a sense, destiny. It means actively pursuing spiritual awareness and evolution, and walking purposefully down our own evolutionary path. It may also mean beginning the journey of coming to terms with and ultimately fulfilling your life's purpose here on earth.

Having some understanding of where you are *now* on your evolutionary path is a great way to begin to develop a barometer for *where you are going* and to see *the steps you need to begin to take to walk your path more consciously.*

YOUR EVOLUTIONARY PATH

Close your eyes and exhale deeply.
Let your shoulders drop.

Rotate your head gently and loosely until you find a comfortable,
balanced position for your head, neck, and shoulders.
Let your jaw relax and hang loose.
Relax your lips, tongue, and throat.
Exhale deeply again and let go.
Continue to breathe easily, slowly, evenly, and deeply.

Allow your mind to clear of all thoughts, and spend a few moments
just focusing on your breathing . . .
breathing easily and deeply . . .
breathing relaxation in when you inhale and breathing away any
tension when you exhale . . .
breathing relaxation into your mind when you inhale and breathing
away any thoughts.

Next, mentally travel through your whole body, relaxing each part
in turn.
Starting with the muscles of your face, then your neck and
shoulders, relax all the way down to your feet and toes.

Remember what it feels like to be in your state of deep relaxation.
Remember your landmarks, and begin to gently re-create those
inside yourself.

Allow yourself to experience your internal stillness, silence, and
serenity.

From a place of deep peace and relaxation, allow yourself to begin
to find a symbol for where you are in your life right now.

You may see a color or an image, feel a physical sensation, hear a
sound or even a voice in your head, or just have a sense of
knowing where you are in your personal journey—
On your personal path . . .

Allow yourself to sensualize . . .

You may want to look back down your path to see where you have
come from . . .

You may want to look forward to see what lies ahead . . .

But the important learning is to understand where you are *now*.

Bring that experience back with you when you reawaken from your
meditation.

Make a note of what your symbol was, so that you can remember it
as you move forward in your personal evolution.
You may wish to check back, over time, to see how you relate to this
symbol—whether your path has remained the same or changed,
and how you are developing on it.

*This might be an appropriate time for you to spend some time alone
with your notebook, diary, or journal. When you begin to open up
the awareness of your life's process in your theta waves, a number of
thoughts, ideas, memories, feelings, or issues may start to arise.
Giving voice to them in writing not only helps to clarify the
knowledge and understanding you have gained by looking inside
yourself, it also helps you to place landmarks along the way so
these ideas and issues may be revisited at a later time more readily,
and it helps you consolidate and ground what it is that you have
learned. It also helps to keep the theta waves more available to you
for future use and development (an example of content helping
develop state).*

*In your journaling, you may wish to actually look back down
your life's path—a short distance or even all the way back to birth.
Notice the high points, the low points, and the junctures in the road,
the crossroads that became turning points.*

What would have happened if you had taken another path at a particular junction? What have you learned that is important to your personal evolution by following the path that you did? What were the overwhelmingly meaningful events that took place along your path?

With these ideas freshly in mind, close your journal and your eyes, and allow yourself to go back down into another meditation.

Slide right back down where you came from, using your landmarks as signposts to help you find your way down.

Check to make sure your body is relaxed and your mind is clear . . .
Take the time that you need to enter your meditation state.

■ ■ ■

Allow yourself to look once again at where you are on your personal evolutionary path.
Review the images or symbols you found in the last meditation to help you again clarify your experience.

Also use the journaling you have just done to look down your path and see even more clearly where you have come from . . .
. . . and how that has led to where you are now.

Now, allow yourself to look *forward* on your path . . .
to see what is ahead of you in more detail than before.

You may see it symbolically,
You may see it metaphorically,
You may feel it in your body,
You may hear it in sounds or even words,
Or it may just be a sense of knowing . . .
what lies ahead.

You may see into the far distance,
missing the link in between now and then.
You may see only a short way ahead.

It may be blurred and hazy
Or it may be more clear than the real thing.

You may even see, with true clarity, blocks or issues up ahead that
you will eventually have to deal with in order to truly proceed
with your own personal evolution.

You may possibly see the path divide, with two potential outcomes
ahead of you.
If so, imagine a journey down each branch of your path.

Spend as long as you like now just meditating on your personal
evolutionary path,
From your far-distant past to your far-distant future,
And be aware of what it is revealing to you . . .

■ ■ ■

Before you close your meditation, there is one more vital phase to it.

Return to where you are right now on your path.
This present moment . . .
This point in time in your personal evolution . . .

Become very still, centered, and present . . .

Allow yourself to become aware of what the very next step on your
own evolutionary path should be.

Is this a small step or a big leap for you?
Is this something you are ready for,

or will it take some time and preparation?
Is this something you look forward to,
or have hesitation or even resistance about?
Is this something you want to do soon,
or something you would prefer to wait for?

What needs to happen in order for you to be ready to take this next
step on your evolutionary path?

Allow yourself to see that happening.
Sensualize it with as many senses as possible.
What it looks like . . .
what it feels like . . .
what it sounds like . . .
to take this next step
successfully and completely.

Spend as long as you like meditating on taking this next step in your
own personal evolution.

■   ■   ■

When you feel ready to close your meditation, make sure that you
find landmarks, images, and symbols, so that you can find your
way back here easily and quickly when you want to.

*As you reemerge from your meditation, bring the images and the
landmarks back with you, and return to your journal, adding these
experiences in whatever detail you wish.*

IDENTIFICATION OF THE BLOCKS

Do you ever feel that you just can't quite make it? Or that no matter
how hard you try, there always seems to be something that gets in

your way? Perhaps you have had the feeling that there is something intangible that almost seems to be slowing down your personal progress—that you really "ought" to be farther ahead and can't quite figure out why you aren't. Or, *"if only . . . ,"* everything would be different.

We all encounter **blocks** along our personal paths. By "block," I mean anything that slows our progress, clouds our vision, or impedes our continuing advancement. This may touch any or all aspects of our lives. It may be in the professional arena, leaving us feeling that "job satisfaction" is always just out of reach. You may experience it in the physical, dogged by a continuing series of health issues. You may feel it most in the emotional or interpersonal areas of your life; or you may even experience a sense of stagnation or stalling in your spiritual awakening.

No matter which area or areas of your personal path seem to have some sort of a block, meditation can begin to help you not only identify the source of the block, but also help you begin the process of clearing it away so that aspect of your life can be more fulfilling, or run more smoothly, or progress at a speedier and steadier rate.

HAVING FAITH IN THE TAO . . .

The philosophy of Taoism is about recognizing and accepting the natural order of things. Finding the way or the path and working with it rather than against it is not necessarily as easy as it may sound. We want to be able to find the flow of energy that moves us through our lives in the best possible way.

This is not about being passive—taking the juice or action out of a given situation. On the contrary, it is about raising your energy level to an appropriate amount and allowing that energy to flow in the *right* way for the given situation. This may mean anything from taking extreme action to resting in inaction until the time is right to move. Being in your Tao means knowing *when* the time is right for action and *what* kind of action to take.

When you are truly in your Tao, this knowing is effortless, automatic. It simply appears obvious to you. The path is laid out in front of you, and you simply have to walk down it. "Trying" becomes an effort that gets in the way, and watching anxiously for results perhaps steers us in the wrong direction.

> The Tao is what *is*—the natural order of things.

Efforting to change that natural order only causes resistance, while passively waiting for it to happen to you can slow down appropriate progress almost to a grinding halt instead of allowing things to move quickly and easily in a swift and suitable flow of right action.

By all means, you must put thought, energy, and focus on things for them to develop in the best possible way—you cannot wait for it to just happen to you. But your focus should be on finding what action is right and natural and correct for your particular path. **This is mastery.**

Part of what can help you to do this is unblocking the blocks on your personal path—so that the flow of energy that is right and appropriate is available to you instead of being obscured by clouded vision, ulterior motives, or emotional debris. Meditation can be a great assistance in this process.

Before the path can be cleared and the road ahead made more available to you, you must first become *aware* of the blocks and pitfalls ahead. Perhaps you have already encountered them and know how they got there, what they mean, and even what you need to do to move on through or beyond them. Then, all that is left is to go ahead and *do it*. In the next chapter, we will look at healing the blocks, overcoming the inertia, and moving forward in a conscious way.

But what if you are stuck and don't even know what the blocks are? How can we begin to identify *what needs to be healed, or what needs to be overcome, or what needs to be transformed* in order for our evolution to continue appropriately on our own personal path. We might spend hours, weeks, or even years thinking about it in beta or discussing it with a partner, friends, or even a therapist. This may or may not prove useful to us. If we stay in beta, the answer invariably remains hidden or limited at best. We need to dip down into our own subconscious, into our theta waves, to really uncover the depth of our inner developmental and evolutionary needs.

The following meditation will begin to help you contact and understand *that which is inside you that needs to heal, change, or transform.* The actual process of *healing* will continue to be addressed in the next chapter.

FINDING THE BLOCK

Find a comfortable, safe meditation space in which to sit or recline.
Close your eyes and begin to enter the state of physical relaxation
and mental stillness that you have already learned in this book.

Become aware of your breathing, allowing your focused detachment
to help take you deeper into your meditation state.
Allow yourself to go through a complete physical relaxation from
the top of your head to the bottom of your feet,
using your breathing as a tool to relax each part of you as you focus
your awareness on it.

Clear your mind of all thoughts and expectations, simply becoming
open, clear, and present.

As you continue to concentrate on your breathing, stimulate alpha
by rolling your eyes upward slightly with either the inhalation or
the exhalation and then downward again on the opposite side of
the cycle.

If you feel you may lose connection with your conscious mind as
you go down into even deeper meditation, stimulate the alpha
bridge even more by sensualizing a healing environment in
which to meditate.

Use as many senses as possible for the greatest effect.
See it, feel it, hear it, smell it, touch it, taste it . . .
experience it in all its many complexities and dimensions . . .

Then settle even more comfortably into it, and allow your
meditation to deepen within you.

Sink down *inside* to the most profound depths . . .

(Add theta-deepening images here if needed—again, refer to
Chapter Three to see how to recall this state, if necessary.)

From this place of depth and relaxation inside yourself, begin to
allow yourself to become aware of the block or blocks that
impede your evolutionary path.

If there are more than one, allow the most important one to present
itself in the foreground of your space of consciousness.

You may see an image . . .
Hear a sound or voice in your head . . .
Have a body sensation . . .
Or even experience a taste, smell, or texture . . .
Or maybe it's just a sense of knowing
that the block is there.

The object of this part of the meditation is to take the block from
being isolated within the deep subconscious up closer to the
conscious border by bringing it also into alpha.

To do this, allow yourself to wrap images or senses around it . . .
Give it form . . . structure . . . shape . . . dimension . . . sound . . .
feel . . . taste or smell.

*This makes it more tangible, more real, and therefore
ultimately more available for transformation. (It is much harder
for us to transform something of which we are not aware or of
which we are only dimly or conceptually aware.) The more we
can concretize the image, the easier it will be to work with.*

*Some blocks present themselves only vaguely and dimly at
first. If this is the case, there are a number of questions you
can ask yourself inside that will help to give alpha form to the
block.*

*Don't worry about the meaning or sense of the answers right
now. The purpose of this is simply to bring the "block" from the
subconscious mind up toward the conscious mind.*

To give it form and tangibility you might ask:

Is it large or small?
Does it have a color?
Is it hot or cold?
Is it wet or dry?
What texture is it?
(Is it rough or smooth?)
Does it have a smell?
. . . a taste?
Does it make a sound?
Does it have a voice?
If so, what does it want to say?
Learn all you can in this way about the block.

The block may present itself to you in other ways.

It may be very tangible, such as an inner child that needs to be healed or an emotional part of you that represents, for example, fear or anger.

It may appear to be circumstantial, as an experience or event in your past that created some sort of trauma. If this is the case, become aware of yourself in those circumstances.

Or it may be very literal. You may see a big brick wall, large boulder, steep cliff, bottomless pit, deep ocean, or black hole. These literal blocks can also easily be worked with.

All you need to do in this meditation is get in touch with the block. *You don't need to do anything with it—simply become aware. You may find that this simple awareness process itself begins the healing, so that by the time you get to the transformative processes in the next chapter, the block will have already moved somewhat. But that is not our intention here. All that we are looking for now is to simply access the material of the subconscious.*

As long as we can begin to make the subconscious become conscious, we can work with that material and begin to learn from it, heal it, or transform it so that we can indeed move through it and take the next step on our evolutionary path.

You may want to again write in your journal or make note in some way of the blocks that you encountered, so that you can refer to this as you move forward in the next chapter to work with healing and transformation.

HEALING THE BLOCKS

*Using Brain-Wave Development and Mastery
for Personal Transformation and Change*

Once we have really begun to investigate our own inner landscape and begun to navigate the terrain of our internal
make-up, we can begin to affect changes inside. Self-exploration,
self-understanding, and self-transformation all can go hand in hand.
You don't need to wait until you understand yourself perfectly and
have a complete and accurate picture of what you feel is ultimately
the most healthy *you* in order to begin to work on healing.

This work can take place in giant leaps and bounds or in little
baby steps or, most likely, in a combination of those two. But it is always a process of learning to take the right "next step," whatever
that may be.

As always, the next best step can be taken most effectively if you
are in your optimum brain-wave state. This gives you the maximum
opportunity for creating and sustaining inner change. You may want
to review the first three chapters and reflect on whether there seem
to be any "holes" in your basic brain-wave training. Or simply check
in with the following simplified correlation table.

BRAIN-WAVE CHECKLIST

- When you begin your meditation, do you have difficulty stilling your mind?

- As your meditation progresses, is your experience interrupted with thoughts of everyday life that are irrelevant to the meditation topic?

- If you are doing a working meditation, do you try to "figure out" the solution rather than allowing it to arise naturally or spontaneously?

- Are you frequently distracted by external stimuli (i.e., the sound of traffic, the energies of other people in the house, the smell of food cooking, etc.)?

- Do you have anxieties or worries that pop in unsolicited?

- Is there sometimes a repetitive low-grade distraction or concern that you can't seem to eliminate?

Any or all of the above are indications that you may be producing unnecessary beta brain waves during your alpha and theta meditation state. Refer back to Chapter One for practice of beta mastery.

- Do you have little or no sensory imagery? (Remember sensory images are not just visual but may be auditory, tactile, gustatory, olfactory, and kinesthetic as well.)

- When you try to image, do you only "think the experience"?

- Are your images only inconsistently present and fleeting, popping in irregularly and unreliably?

- Are your images consistently present but dim and hazy or overly dark?

- Do you lose conscious awareness when you meditate?

- Do you think you are going to remember your experience during the meditation itself, but after it is over, you have lost recall?

If you answer yes to the above, you are most likely not producing or perhaps not sustaining enough alpha brain waves. Refer to Chapter Two for increasing alpha development.

- Do you have a sense that you are only scratching the surface?

- Do you feel your answers or insights are not coming from deep within you?

- Do you still crave more profundity in your meditations?

- Do you feel there is something deep inside just waiting to be released?

- Do you sense a lack in your spiritual connection?

If any of these are the case, you may want to review your theta brain-wave development in Chapter Three.

I want to emphasize that your brain waves do not need to be completely developed or under your mastery in order to strongly benefit from the following meditations. In fact, the meditations in these chapters will assist the continuing evolution and awakening of all of your brain waves. However, if you feel like you have a particular deficiency or problem in one area, you may want to practice

specific development of that brain wave concurrently with the healing meditations.

These meditations will automatically help you in adding the beta brain waves back to the alpha, theta, and delta to create an awakened mind as explained in Chapter Four.

HOW DO YOU WANT IT TO BE?

If there is one overriding principle in learning how to make inner change and transformation, it is to find out how you are experiencing things right now and then ask yourself the question, "How do I want it to be?" This question can be effective in many forms:

- "What do I want it to look like?"

- "How do I want it to feel?"

If applicable, you can use any or all of the other senses . . .

- "What does it smell like now, and how do I want it to smell?"

- "What does it taste like now, and how do I want it to taste?"

- "What does it sound like now, and how do I want it to sound?"

- "What is its texture now, and how would I like it to feel when I touch it?"

The most basic questions to answer are, "What am I experiencing inside now?" and, "What do I want this experience inside to be?" *Then use your powers of imagery and your meditation ability to create that experience.*

TRANSFORMING THE BLOCK

As we will see later, the dialoguing can get much more complex, but for now, let's practice these simple changes from A to B (change what it is now to what you want it to be). To do this, let's go back to the meditation in the previous chapter on finding the block. (See page 165.)

You may remember your experience and wish to apply it here, or you may wish to try this meditation again now with the specific idea of looking at an inner block using questions like the following. (Add your own to personalize this even more.)

Is it large or small?

Does it have a color?

Is it hot or cold?

Is it wet or dry?

What texture is it?

(Is it rough or smooth?)

Does it have a smell?

. . . a taste?

Does it make a sound?

Now suppose you have identified your block, or that which needs healing, as: "small, red, hot, dry, rough, putrid smelling and tasting, with a grating, high-pitched sound." Then your task would be to go inside and find out what size, color, temperature, texture, etc., you most want it to be for optimum transformation. So it may end up as: "large, blue, cool, moist, smooth, and sweet, with a low, melodious gong sound."

Meditating in this way, we are beginning to make inner change without necessarily contacting or dealing with specific content. Some inner issues or blockages may effectively be healed this way without ever really knowing any more about what this represents to you.

A CHILD'S STORY

This method of inner transformation and healing works especially well for those who have little or no beta understanding of the source of their problem and who prefer not to or have difficulty with involving their analytical minds in the healing process. It works almost exclusively with metaphor and symbolism. Communicating with and transforming the subconscious in this way is especially useful with children.

I was working with a fifth-grade child named Jennifer. Her parents had brought her to me because she was having a very hard time in school, failing her lessons, unhappy, and acting out at home. She had already been held back a grade in school and yet was unable to keep up with her classmates. The fact that she was expected to progress to middle school at the end of the year was very daunting to her.

I asked her to describe to me what it felt like when she was unhappy and "bouncing off the walls," as she liked to refer to it. Through a series of questions, we identified that when she was feeling bad, her physical sensation was "tight skin," the color she saw was "red," the temperature was "hot," the emotion was "sad," and she experienced having "tense eyes."

I asked her, "What would it be like if you felt good?" and her reply was, "Happy, cool, blue, loose skin, relaxed eyes." As she repeated those words over and over, her brain waves gradually organized, stabilized, and improved. We turned those words into her "personal mantra." Every time she felt unhappy or that she was having difficulty in school, she repeated her mantra and tried to re-create the sensation she felt when her brain waves were in their optimum state. Her parents and

teacher were not only intrigued but supportive of her new "meditation
practice."

The time I spent working with Jennifer paid off. Her D and F grades
became As and Bs, and I will never forget the pride with which she
brought me her fifth-grade report card. She passed with flying colors and
progressed to middle school feeling successful and triumphant.

Another deeper and more complex way of working with personal transformation and healing is to find out in a more content-
specific way what the block represents. This is an awakened mind
developing meditation by virtue of the need to add beta to the meditation pattern. You can begin to develop a more meaningful type of
dialogue with the inner part of yourself by giving it a voice and finding out what it has to say.

The following meditation picks up after you have identified the
block and are ready to begin dialoguing with it.

TRANSFORMING THE BLOCK

How is this block part feeling?

How long has it been there?

How did it get there?

What does it need or want from you?

What role or purpose does it play in your life?

What is its *positive purpose*? In other words, how does it serve
   you?

What needs to happen for the block to heal . . .

or the transformation that you are seeking to occur?

How does this part feel about this change occurring?

Now allow that transformation to begin to occur inside you.

Experience what it looks like . . . what it feels like . . . what it
sounds like . . . even what it smells and tastes like . . . for this block
to be transformed or healed in the way that it needs to be.

Use as many of your senses as possible to imagine the change taking
place. Look into the future. Sensualize yourself in the future after
this transformation has already taken place.

Experience what it looks like . . . what it feels like . . . what it sounds
like . . . even what it smells and tastes like . . . for this block to be
transformed or healed in the way that you want it to be.

Live the experience.

*When you are ready to complete your meditation, spend a few minutes
inside preparing to close. Crystallize your experience in a few key images, words, or phrases. Bring those out with you when you awaken from
your meditation. As always, verbalizing, talking into a tape recorder,
telling a friend, or writing down what happened will fix the experience
firmly in your conscious beta mind so that it will remain present for you
and not slip back into your subconscious.*

*Make sure that you stretch, breathe deeply, and arouse properly before
you leave your meditation space.*

As you continue your path of self-healing by delving into secondary gain,
please be aware that *some illnesses or disease processes are completely
unavoidable.* They may be part of your genetics, they may be congenital,
or they may be environmental. While there is always something to be
gained by looking at the positive purpose of an illness, never allow your
investigation to lead to self-blame.

Secondary Gain

Before we continue with healing the blocks, we need to address a very important element of the healing process that may be relevant to you. If your block or problem has a hidden benefit or a positive purpose, that can be called **secondary gain**. If you ask yourself, "How is this block serving me?" you may find the secondary gain involved.

Examples of secondary gain range from the common experience of getting sick on the day of a big exam in school (the gain is not having to take the exam), to receiving the love and attention you never got from your spouse after you contract cancer (the gain is love and attention), to repressing the memory of a traumatic childhood event (the gain is self-protection from pain and anguish), to being unable to move forward in your career for fear of failure (the gain is preventing anxiety).

THE "NEW AGE" DILEMMA

We need to be careful here when we are dealing with illness, lest we go overboard with self-responsibility. A common question among those in the "New Age" self-healing circles is, "Why did I cause that?" or "Why do I need that illness?" We're walking a fine edge here. On one hand, *everything* that happens to us can be thought of as our responsibility as seen over lifetimes of the evolution of the spirit, ranging from "Why did I choose *these* parents?" on up. On the other hand, we can get into a potential danger zone if we try to read hidden meaning and responsibility into every aspect of our health and well-being.

I believe in the theory of germs! It is quite possible to catch an illness because we are standing next to a person who transmits it to us. However, the sincerely dedicated might ask, "Why did I need that germ at that particular time?" One answer might be, "I was working too hard and got run down, and therefore I was more susceptible to the germ than I would normally have been." In the same vein one might ask, "Do I perhaps need this illness as a reason to take a few days off from work so I can get some rest? Would it instead be possible to take those days off from work *before* I get ill and thereby prevent the illness?" If we can find the hidden agenda or positive purpose in the illness and find another way of solving the problem without getting sick, then the illness might be avoided altogether.

Along the same line, if we simply try to heal the problem without looking for the root cause, we may be successful only for a time. Soon, a new problem or block pops up out of the same root cause. We might stop smoking cigarettes only to develop an eating disorder. We might heal the nausea but develop an ulcer until we find out what it is in our life that we "can't stomach."

I work on a basic principle that all parts of a human being are working in some way for the good of the whole, no matter how misguided they may be.

The root cause of a problem may initially appear to be negative—often a form of punishment. If you do this work, it is essential that you track the negative aspects of your problem back to their original positive purpose. Let's look at a few examples of this process to get a deeper understanding of how it works.

TWO EXAMPLES OF HEALING

1. A man has a severe case of eczema. He goes into deep meditation and contacts the part of himself that is responsible for causing the disfiguring skin condition. He sees an image of an ugly scaly face and asks it what the purpose of the eczema is. His inner part says, "To make you ugly." We cannot stop here. This is not a positive purpose. He asks, "What is the positive purpose in me being ugly?" "To keep you from going out with women!" "What is the positive purpose of keeping me from going out with women?" "To keep you from getting married." Still not a positive purpose. "What is the positive purpose of keeping me from getting married?" *"To protect*

you from being abandoned!" This individual experienced abandonment by his mother as a young child. As a result, his psyche had been trying to protect him from a repeat of that experience. At last, we have found our *positive* purpose.

With this knowledge, he can then decide for himself whether or not he still feels the need for this kind of protection. His parents had a painfully broken marriage resulting in his mother leaving, and his inner psyche was simply doing its best to protect him from having that experience himself. He may be able to work through his feelings about marriage and realize that he no longer needs protection from it. Or he may still feel that he doesn't want to get married, but with that knowledge now available to him on a conscious level, he might choose more appropriate ways of maintaining his unmarried status. He no longer needs the protection of the eczema.

> As you uncover the positive purposes in your blocks, remember that almost all secondary gain revolves in some way around self-protection.

Again, I want to stress that you should only look for the positive purpose or secondary gain of an illness if you are drawn to that way of working. For others, the idea that the illness is somehow serving them feels inappropriate and unrelated to their situation. In that case, they may prefer to sensualize healing as in Transforming the Block above. As always, follow your instincts. Do not try to force secondary gain to exist where there is none.

All of these principles apply to "healing" (transforming, developing, evolving) any aspect of our being—whether it be physical, mental, emotional, or spiritual. This is why I use the concept of "block." That term can refer to *anything* that is getting in the way of our optimum well-being in any area.

2. A woman wants to know why she has uncontrollable fear whenever she gets in the shower. Looking for the block inside, she finds a

large stone wall (literally a "block"). Dialoguing with the wall, she discovers it is protecting her from learning information that the wall feels she is incapable of handling. After she assures the wall that she is ready and prepared for anything, she is allowed to see on the other side of it. There she finds a large mountain (another block). Dialoguing with the mountain, she understands that her psyche really wants her to prepare carefully for the information she is going to receive if she laboriously journeys to the other side of the peak. Weeks of work and preparation allow her to finally regain the memories that have been repressed. As a child, she was severely molested by a neighbor while taking a shower. Although she had buried the memory, her subconscious had prevented her from taking a shower ever since, for fear of it happening again. Having dealt with the memory and the abuse itself, she is now able to easily take showers, although she still prefers the bathtub.

It is important that this work be done on a theta brain-wave level. For permanent changes to take place within the subconscious, the subconscious has to be accessed. By just thinking about the problem and talking about it in beta, it is difficult for effective or permanent healing to take place.

The following meditation deals with the issue of secondary gain and provides a framework for any meditation on self-healing and personal transformation. This can also be classed as an awakened-mind meditation, a "working" meditation, and one that adds the beta brain waves back to the meditation pattern.

HEALING THE BLOCK

- Before you begin, consider what you want to look for inside. Is there a specific block of which you are already aware?

- Still your mind and relax your body. Let go of any preconceptions and expectations of any particular solution or outcome.

- Create a framework of imagery for yourself to meditate within in order to access alpha waves (i.e., an outdoor sanctuary, a meditation room, a healing space, etc.).

- Take your meditation deeper—go deeply *inside yourself* to create theta waves.

- Very gently and easily begin to allow yourself to get in touch with the block inside that needs healing.

- Find some way to manifest this part as clearly as you can— some way to connect with it. This may take the form of a symbol, image, color, body sensation, even taste or smell, or it may just be a sense of knowing that the part is there. It's not important to have a crystal-clear image of that part. The more clearly you can bring it into focus, the easier it will be for you to communicate with this part of yourself later on. At this stage of the meditation, however, do the best you can. All you really need is to connect with the sense of knowing that the part exists inside you.

- Begin to internally dialogue with it, so that you can make further connection and get information. You can ask it if it is willing to communicate with you. If the answer is "yes," proceed. If the answer is "no," ask this part what needs to take place to allow you to communicate. If there is no answer, proceed as if the answer had been "yes." You may hear the answers in words. You may experience them as images or sense them through body sensations, or it may just be a kind of a "knowing." Remember to trust what you are sensing.

- Dialogue with this part of yourself. You might begin by asking, "How are you feeling?" Let this part express itself to you in whatever form it is able. You might want to ask, "How long have you been there?" or "What do you need?"

Continue to dialogue with this subconscious part of
yourself to get closer to it, to understand why it is doing
what it is doing.

· Next you might ask, "What role do you play in my life?"
"What is your positive purpose for me?" or "How do you
serve me?" You may also find your own specific questions.
Take some time on your own to continue your exploration.

· Express your appreciation to this part. Because it has been
working *for* you, it deserves recognition and appreciation
even if it has ultimately (and unintentionally) caused you
harm.

*(This step may be hard for some people. They may have so much
anger at a part that has been blocking their progress that it is hard to
understand that the reason for the block has been self-protection or
survival. Have faith here that your subconscious, although misguided,
has your best intentions at heart. Giving it appreciation for those intentions does not mean condoning its continuing use of its methods.)*

· Now, explain to this part how *you* are feeling. *Even if your
conscious mind realizes fully how this part has been blocking
you or is detrimental to you, don't expect your subconscious
mind to understand without careful explanation.* Don't
blame. Use all of the communication skills you would use
with another human being. Tell the part how its behavior
has been affecting you (i.e., what having the block has
meant to you and the difficulties it has created).

· Consider what you would like to have happen now. Look at
the original reason for the block. Do you still need it, or has
that need changed? What do you actually want your
subconscious to do?

- Tell your subconscious what you want. Ask it to help you get what you need for yourself right now. If necessary, remind it that it is here to benefit you, and what it has been doing in the past no longer serves you.

- Negotiate. Actually bargain with your subconscious. You can continue to use questions to help you with this communication. If you still need the *role* that this part plays to be active within you (for example, for protection or survival), ask if it can fulfill this role in a different way—one that would no longer require you to experience the negative side-effect of the block. If you no longer need this service, tell it that, and ask if it would be willing to stop doing it. Useful questions also might be "What would it take for you to stop blocking me?" or "What needs to happen to make a change for the better?"

- Come to a deal with your subconscious. Perhaps you need to put it in a time frame or within some other context in your life; i.e., "If I _____, then you will allow this block to dissolve."

- Thank this part for its willingness to cooperate. Again, treat it like an honored and respected friend.

- Prepare for closure. Ask your subconscious part if there is anything else that it wants to communicate to you right now. Tell it any final things you would like to tell it before you complete your meditation. You may want to make plans to check back with the subconscious material at a specified time in the future to see if this transformation is still working or if there are any unforeseen problems that have arisen.

- Complete your meditation and reawaken taking several deep rapid breaths and stretching fully.

- Ground the meditation by putting it into words—writing it down or talking about it.

This meditation can be applied to any problem, difficulty, or issue that needs transformation or healing by simply altering what you are choosing to work on. Allow yourself to find a way to manifest the issue or problem through sensualization. Find a symbol, an image, a body sensation, a feeling, a sound, or even a voice in your head. Or it could simply be a sense of knowing that the part that needs healing is present. Then you can begin your dialogue with that part of you and continue the rest of the meditation.

BREAKTHROUGH IN THE WOMB

One woman reports that she is aware of the exact moment a life-altering change took place in the middle of practicing this meditation. Her history is somewhat complex, so I will only touch on the salient points. Rebecca had started therapy at the age of 24 when she realized that she "did not know the meaning of the word joy." After years of therapy, she found some "brief but fleeting glimpses of joy." The end of a relationship at 37 caused a long-term depression to set in again. By 41, she was able to stop being suicidal, but the depression was still present, the desire to live was not strong, and the joy was still elusive.

At 48, she learned about this work, and at 49, she was in the middle of practicing this meditation when she had a "life-altering breakthrough." She was aware that at some point in her past she had made a decision that, in her words, was, "OK. I'm going to live, but I'm not going to be happy." She had been carrying that unhappiness for decades.

Rebecca "became aware that this particular block had been plaguing me for years and was underlying everything." During this particular meditation, she went back to her experience inside her mother's womb. She remembered being inundated with an "onslaught of biochemistry energy" from her mother's difficult life experience and relationships. She remembered the point at which she made the decision, "OK. I'm going to live, but I'm not going to be happy about it."

At this point in the meditation, she started differentiating between "me" and "not me," actually using her hands and arms to sort through and throw out that which was "not me"—the unhappiness. She finally experienced herself in the womb as being happy and found that she could remake the choice she had made. Now she was going to live *and* be happy. Within a couple of days, she experienced "an automatic repelling of all energies coming in that were 'not me.'" She uses the kinesthetic landmark of the sensation of her hands and arms blocking and throwing away everything that is "not me" to give herself a continuing strong sense of who she actually is. As a result of that breakthrough, she now "feels whole and balanced and alive and ready to embrace life."

EMOTIONAL WOUNDS AND SCARS

We are all invariably heir to *some* amount of emotional wounding as our lives unfold from childhood to maturity. The scars from these wounds run more or less deeply depending on the nature and the extent of the original damage, the amount of subsequent healing that has occurred, and whether or not the injury has continued to reoccur due to similar circumstances. In fact, some childhood injuries are so pervasive and extensive that they begin to feel familiar and almost comfortable to the child. This is the only life he knows; this is what he has come to expect. Or even, this is what he has begun to equate with love because the perpetrator of the abuse is someone who ostensibly loved him.

So what can easily happen in these situations is that the child actually actively (albeit subconsciously) seeks the re-creation of these wounds on into adulthood. The original trauma continues again and again, perhaps only in slightly different forms, as the subconscious seeks one or both of two things: the repetition of something familiar and therefore somehow comforting, even if horrific; and/or the ability to finally create a different ending, to heal as an adult that which was impossible to stop as a child.

Unfortunately, that healing often cannot occur while the individual is still unconscious of the original trauma. A new ending is rarely possible when the cast of characters, the plot, and the action are the same, even if the actors and the stage setting are different. The old, familiar groove is too deep and ingrained when the main actor (the abused or wounded) doesn't know about or understand the need for his or her behavior or defense mechanisms to be *consciously* changed to create a new and *permanently different* ending.

If you can make the subconscious become conscious by bringing the information where it is stored in theta up through alpha to your conscious beta mind, then you will have access to that original wounding and programming for subsequent similar wounds. Then the decision to heal can be made by your aware conscious mind (in beta). That new information (decision for change) can then be sent back down into the subconscious so that the early wound can be healed or at least salved, and the repetitive behavior can cease. <u>In this way, inner transformation can occur, and the individual can continue on his or her evolutionary path.</u>

Through meditation, it is possible to go inside, back to the original childhood wound, and begin to facilitate that healing process. This will ultimately result in a transformation of current behavior so that it is no longer based on playing out the childhood trauma. This is simply a specific application of the above generic meditation.

INNER CHILD WORK

Much has been made of **inner child work** over the last several years. It is a valuable form of healing that can be made even more effective by combining it with understanding the appropriate brain-wave states in which to carry it out. Talking in a beta brain-wave state with your inner child might be an interesting exercise, but it will reveal no more to you than that which your conscious mind is already aware of. Good therapists have the ability to "talk you down" into theta brain waves to access the deeper subconscious states where the wounded inner child lingers.

Through meditation, you can begin to access these states and the content of your wounded inner child, if indeed you have one, by yourself. As always, it is useful to have pen and paper for journaling and making notes to help you remember important points and ground your experience.

If you have already worked in any therapeutic process or consciously contacted any childhood wounds, traumas, or repetitive negative behavior patterns, take a few minutes to consider these. Outline in your mind (or on paper) what it is you already know and what it is that you would like to heal. Stirring things up consciously in this way will help give the subconscious a "kick start" with content so that you can home in on the right area of work during the meditation.

If you have a particular wound or pattern that you would like to heal or change, now is a good time to identify that. You may find that, when you do the meditation, you will end up working on something completely different or perhaps a deeper layer of the same thing, but it is always very valuable to have a starting point. This kind of conscious reverie gives you a place of content to start from in your meditation. If you do not have any idea where to start, you may either return to the meditation Finding the Block, or just simply trust that this meditation will reveal to you that which you need to know for the next step in your healing.

Once you have done all the conscious (beta) work you wish to do, put down your writing materials and prepare yourself for meditation. Find a comfortable place to sit or lie down where you won't be disturbed. You may wish to play some gentle and *very* soft music in the background. (Be careful that it is not too melodious or loud to distract your attention from your inner journey, only a soft bed of sound on which to rest as you relax down.) Give yourself at least half an hour to complete this meditation.

INNER CHILD MEDITATION

Begin with at least ten minutes of deep relaxation.

Sensualize a healing environment.
This helps develop alpha waves.

Now, find a comfortable place to sit within this environment, and
    allow yourself to go into a very deep meditation . . .

Allow yourself to use all of the tools you have learned so far to go
    down into a deep state of alpha and theta . . .
It might be a sense of falling
. . . down
. . . sliding
. . . down
. . . drifting
. . . down
Deep within yourself . . .

As you begin to withdraw, deeply, profoundly, into yourself . . .
. . . away from the external environment
. . . away from any surrounding sounds or stimuli
You may begin to feel a sensation almost as if the very boundaries of
    your body are becoming hazy
. . . vague.

Almost as if the boundaries of your body cease to exist
and you have become one with your consciousness,
there inside,
deep inside,
in the very depths of your innermost being,
your essence.

And here in the deep peace and tranquility of your innermost
    being,
you can very gently begin to get in touch
with that wounded inner child . . .
with the inner child with whom you need to spend time
deep inside . . .
that inner child part of you
that may still need healing.

And you can begin to get an image
that represents this child . . .
or a sensation,
or sense of knowing
what it feels like,
what it looks like,
what it sounds like
to be this child
inside.

And ask this child now to be willing to communicate with you.
Let him or her know that you are here to help . . .
and to heal.

And begin to allow yourself to ask this child how it is feeling.
And let the child respond to you however it wishes and however it
    can.

If it is physically weak, frail, or vulnerable, you may need to
administer "first aid" or make him or her physically comfortable
before you can move on.

If the child is frightened, sad, or emotionally vulnerable,
you may need to reassure him or her . . .

Hold the child, comfort it, and support it in whatever way
you can.
The child may want to sit in your lap for a while,
and you may find it needs to cry while you soothe and console it.

Or the child may be wary . . . even aloof, distant, or disdainful.
In this case, you will need to proceed respectfully and cautiously,
as you would approaching a lost and wary child you found in
public.
While respecting and honoring the child's need for safety and
privacy,
reassure him or her that you are there for the purpose of healing,
and ask your inner child to please let you do that.

If the child is angry, ask why,
and let it storm and rage until it is relieved and released.

Ask your inner child what he or she needs now to feel better, to
heal, and to become whole.

What needs to happen for the child to trust again?
. . . to laugh again?
. . . to be happy?
. . . and to feel safe?

What needs to happen for the child
. . . to feel good about himself or herself?

What needs to happen for the child to heal?

And allow yourself to let these things begin to happen.

■ ■ ■

Give yourself all of the time you need to stay inside
with your inner child . . .
talking, comforting, and healing . . .
supporting, in whatever way you can,
what is wanted and needed . . .
the healing process of your inner child.

■ ■ ■

There may be certain things your inner child would like you to do
in your outside adult life to further facilitate its healing.

Let the child really share its needs, wishes, and hopes with you.
He or she may have waited a long time to be brought to your
conscious mind.
Give it the time it needs now to really communicate what would
help it begin to heal.
And let that healing begin to happen now deep inside . . .

■ ■ ■

Sensualize this healing taking place with as many senses as
possible.

■ ■ ■

If there is something the child asks you to do in your outside adult
world,

be very clear as to whether or not this is truly possible.
If not, explain why and offer an alternative.
If it is at all possible to fulfill your child's needs,
you can make a commitment to do it,
including a time frame within which you will act.
Imagine letting these changes take place in your life.

■   ■   ■

Now allow yourself to look into the future and see your inner child
    as happy, whole, free, independent, safe . . .
. . . and living a full and satisfying life.

And as you look into the future,
notice how this healing changes things for you as an adult.
Perhaps you can see how this healing could rewrite your entire
    future.

■   ■   ■

And in a little while, you're going to begin to find a closure to this
    meditation.
Take the time that you need now to come to completion with your
    inner child . . .
. . . inside.

You may want to find a time to revisit the child later,
especially if you feel you have more work to do with him or her.

■   ■   ■

Bring yourself back in the usual way, grounding the memory of your
    meditation in words . . .

And allow yourself to awaken feeling alert and refreshed,
and ready to move forward in your life.

Following through with any commitments you have made inside is very important, for both the needs of your subconscious and
the continuing development of your mastery. Checking back with
your inner child in a brief follow-up meditation within a day or two
after your initial contact with this subconscious part can keep the
process alive and moving within you. Once you have opened up the
channels to this part of yourself, the landmarks are usually clear and
relatively accessible; and you can reconnect quickly, easily, and frequently. You may want to meditate several times around the same
inner-child issue, or you may even find a number of "inner-
children" with whom you want to communicate.

THE BLANKET OF STARS

John participated in this Inner Child Meditation at a recent workshop at
Esalen Institute. He reported that he saw a three-year-old boy sitting in his
old family house kitchen looking *very* lonely, sad, and disoriented. When
he tried to communicate, the boy ignored him and he felt powerless to help.

John said, "I asked the boy if I could send him blue light, and he,
with a minimal nod, said OK. Then he instantly shifted into a large beam
of blue light emanating from my belly, which carried him up. I was concerned that, since my mother had died when I was two and a half after a
year in great pain, this was opening a 'can of worms' late in the workshop. But later in another meditation, I held and rocked the boy. The next
morning, while I was jogging on the Big Sur road, the boy again ap-
peared in the kitchen scene. I morphed into my mother and went and held
the boy closely on my lap. After a time, I explained to him that I was sorry,
that I had to go to be with God, but that I had a gift for him—a blanket of

stars that contained my love. I surrounded him with the blanket and immediately experienced intense sobbing that racked my body and made jogging impossible. I walked back with more bursts of sobbing. Later, I felt amazingly clear and whole.

"During the last meditation of the workshop, I sat surrounded by my blanket cocoon of luminous blackness and turned up the rheostat. The microscopic, luminous points instantly brightened into shimmering stars and expanded in all directions to become the universe. I was inside-outside [reference to the beta mastery meditation, in Chapter One], and the feeling was of stunning expansion into cosmic love and light. I ended the workshop with a 'Big Bang.' Thank you.

"Since the workshop . . . I feel a deep sense of calmness that is beyond anything that I've had from a retreat. That is particularly wonderful since I don't have a fear of it gradually dwindling away. Along with the calmness is excitement that this journey is only beginning."

CHAPTER
EIGHT

MEDITATION AND THE ENERGY SYSTEM

Awakening the Kundalini

This book is about awakening the mind to mastery through meditation and brain-wave training. We are working with the interplay between the state and the content of consciousness to develop this awakening in the most effective and direct way. We also need to be aware that when we awaken the mind, other changes may take place within the body-mind. One such change that can occur is in the energy system.

The relationship between the awakening of the mind and the awakening of the energy system is apparent. The nervous system, which includes the brain, is very closely linked to the energy system. If we worked long enough on awakening the mind—and therefore the brain—we would ultimately awaken the energy system. Conversely, if we worked long enough on awakening the energy system, we would ultimately awaken the mind. Both are vital in the process of becoming a master and can go hand in hand, although not necessarily simultaneously. They are two ends of the same continuum of our evolutionary process. This energetic development, like its parallel brain-wave development, is becoming a more and more common and accepted phenomenon and experience.

The human species has continued to evolve over centuries and centuries of existence to become what it is today. We would be incredibly short-sighted and egotistical if we were to believe that the human race has come to the end of its evolution—in other words, if it has stopped changing and progressing, adapting to develop and improve as a living organism.

I believe that awakening is an aspect of the process of evolution. This means awakening the mind and awakening the energy system. The process of awakening the energy system has been a well-documented and long-accepted phenomenon within many religious and spiritual traditions. The awakening of the mind to mastery has likewise been accepted; however, it is only recently that we have been able to measure and monitor it scientifically. Only with the advent of the Mind Mirror have we been able to see awakening defined so clearly in terms of brain waves. And therefore, only now do we have this new tool and understanding for training and developing the mind of a master.

As human evolution progresses, there will be some point in the future when we will look back on the "dark ages" of the twenty-first century, when a majority of people did not have an awakened mind, when we couldn't "read each other's minds," when we were not aware of universal consciousness or the collective unconscious, and when our energy systems lay dormant, not yet functioning at full flow and power. In other words, we will look back at a time before we were awakened.

Every spiritual tradition includes some form of awakening that involves the unconscious becoming conscious. When we look at the masters, this awakening shows itself in their brain waves with the combination of beta, alpha, theta, and delta that we call the awakened mind. Here the flow of information between the unconscious, the subconscious, and the conscious mind is complete.

This awakening can also be seen in the energy system in the

form of what is referred to by the ancient tantric texts as **kundalini**. The awakening of kundalini is a kind of rebirth or purification process that is said to mark the first steps toward **enlightenment**—in other words, the unconscious becoming conscious, or the complete expression of mastery.

Kundalini is symbolized in Yoga philosophy as a serpent that lies in the base of the spine in every human being, usually sleeping and yet to be awakened. *Kunda* literally means "bowl" or "basin." Before its awakening, the serpent is coiled in the pelvic bowl. When the energy is released, it moves upward through the spine, giving the individual access to much greater powers and awarenesses than he or she had before. The Chi Kung masters I referred to in Chapter Four use an aspect of this energy for healing others.

The kundalini serpent is the storehouse and spiritual link to a wealth of energy, strength, abilities, and awareness. The activation of kundalini is the *release* of this latent energy into the individual's physical, emotional, mental, and spiritual system, and the beginning of a wide variety of phenomena. When the process is completed, there is greater psychological maturity, emotional balance, personal strength, and spiritual awakening. Because it is a *rebirth,* however, in the initial stages of the process, the individual may experience some of the confusion, helplessness, and unpredictability of a child. The process, then, is one of *allowing* this energy to develop and mature. *You do not create the kundalini energy,* just as you do not create your own life force as a child, but you can "tap into" it, learn to master it, and encourage it on its journey of development.

The process of kundalini awakening is one of "de-stressing" the entire psycho-physical system. In order for this purification to occur, the system has to be cleared of **blocks** in the energy channels so that the energy can flow smoothly, evenly, consistently, and fully throughout. Among the many causes of these blocks are physical disturbances, emotional trauma, illness, diet and nutrition, and mental and psychological belief systems. These can be internal messages carried throughout life, such as, "It's not OK to feel pleasure";

and "Higher spiritual awareness does not exist"; or even, "I am not worthy of awakening."

Think of your body's energy system like a garden hose left outside over the winter. Twigs and dirt have made their way inside. Perhaps there are even small stones or pebbles to block the water's flow. The hose has been kinked in several places, as well as stepped on and crushed. Because you didn't need to water anything in the winter, you haven't been concerned about the hose. If you turned on a trickle of water, it would come out unimpeded.

What happens when you turn the water up full force? The hose flops around until it finds a stable and open position to accommodate the unaccustomed strong flow of water. The blocks are blasted out by the force of the flow, and eventually the stream of water is strong and the hose is fully functioning.

The human energy system, while decidedly more complex, can behave in a similar fashion. When a strong surge of kundalini energy flows through obstructed channels, the body tends to "flop" around just as the hose does, hence the origin of the *kriyas*—yogic "actions" or movements. Yoga was not developed because a master thought with his beta waves, "If I get into that particular position, I will become more awakened or more aware." Yoga was developed because the energy of kundalini flowed in the master's body and moved him into various positions that were later defined as the practice of Yoga. The students, seeing their master in these various positions, thought, "If I get in this position too, then maybe I will become awakened like my master."

The classic kundalini awakening initially involves the rising of energy from the root **chakra** (or energy center) in the perineum. The earliest symptoms are often experienced in the feet, the legs, and the toes—the big toes in particular. As the process continues, the energy rises up through the chakras, clearing any obstructions it finds in its path. As it hits a chakra, it tends to spread out through all of the psycho-physical systems related to that chakra. When the energy encounters a block or resistance and then overcomes it and cleanses the physical, emotional, and psychological systems governed by that chakra, that chakra is considered to be "opened." Theoretically, the energy progresses in sequence, from the root chakra, up to the crown chakra in the top of the head. Then it spreads down across the face and the chest and comes to rest in the navel area. In reality, this orderly progression rarely happens. The energy jumps around from location to location. You may indeed feel it first in the feet and legs, but then feel it next in the throat, before it goes back down to the heart.

The energy may seek out the largest blocks first and work in layers. The cycle of awakening may happen again and again as layers of resistance are overcome and the energy system is more and more refined. The time this process takes is also widely variable. The major portion may be completed in a few years, or it may continue slowly for decades. It is also possible to feel that the process is complete, only to have it recur years later around a new block that has developed or been uncovered, as a subtle experience of fine-tuning. Looking for an end to the experience does no good whatsoever. It is a *process,* not a *goal.*

> The awakening of the spiritual force of kundalini is our birthright as human beings.

SYMPTOMS OF KUNDALINI AWAKENING

There are a wide variety of experiences that are attributed to kundalini. These do not *all* occur to any one person—and they may occur at different times, spaced very far apart. Some people only lightly experience a few of the symptoms yet are still undergoing a kundalini awakening. Some experience one type, and then get a break before experiencing a completely different set. Others may go through the whole range quickly or slowly.

Physical sensations: such as tingling, crawling, or itching on the *inside* of the skin, a feeling of inner vibration, bubbling, or quivering. Because symptoms often begin in the root chakra, in the nerves at the base of the spine, the initial sensations may begin in the lower extremities, frequently the toes.

Body movement: ranging from simple rhythmical swaying or undulation during meditation to more extreme spontaneous Yoga postures as the energy pushes the body into specific positions in its attempt to open up the channels of free flow. Spontaneous stretching can also occur, most frequently in times of rest and repose. You may experience a sense of elongation, especially of the spine and back.

Visual symptoms: range from brief flashes of light inside the head to full-blown, lengthy spiritual visions. One might also experience the "seed of light," a tiny point of light that appears in the third-eye area, between the eyebrows. Sometimes referred to as the "blue pearl," this light will seem to appear between you and anything that you are looking at.

Illumination: Some rare individuals have been known to glow visibly in the dark as a result of this awakening. The halo in religious art is not simply an artist's rendition of a representation of spirituality, but a visible illumination caused by light emanating from the crown chakra and the circle of chakras around the top of the head.

Auditory symptoms: Hearing can become distorted. A wide range of inner sounds can occur, including ringing, hissing, crackling, buzzing, whistling, whooshing, roaring, knocking, ocean sounds, musical notes, or even voices.

Temperature changes: sensations of extreme heat manifesting in two ways: "hot flashes" in the body; or extremities of the body, especially the hands, becoming excessively hot to the touch.

Changes in breathing patterns: Most frequently occurring during meditation, the breathing patterns can range from short, sharp, and shallow to long, extended, slow breaths almost resembling the cessation of breathing.

Emotional swings: During an energetic awakening, there is absolutely no emotion that is off limits or out of bounds. You might experience swings of despair, low self-esteem, fear, anger, or self-doubt, ultimately culminating in sensations of bliss, harmony, peace, and universal joy for increasingly longer periods of time.

Perceptual changes: the sense of growing to great size, expanding beyond your body, or having out-of-body experiences. In a milder form, this state can be experienced as extreme detachment or disassociation.

Changes in sexual energy: Sexual intercourse and/or orgasm can temporarily stimulate and increase the activity of the kundalini energy. After an orgasm, you may feel increased symptoms in any of the categories discussed above, especially body sensations and body movement. The awakening of the kundalini may also stimulate an increased sexual desire. The arousal of the energy itself can feel like an orgasm and can be referred to as a "deep, ecstatic and blissful internal tickle." When it is complete and moves up above the lower sexual chakra, it is experienced as a total body orgasm.

MEDITATION ON THE CHAKRAS

To better understand the kundalini phenomena, we can explore certain aspects of the human energy system. While it is now widely accepted that within the body there are interconnected channels of energy, attitudes about the existence, form, and purposes of these channels vary in accordance with culture, philosophy, medical background, and spiritual orientation. A complete summary of the divergent opinions on this subject is not the purpose of this chapter; however, I would like to offer an overview of the tantric approaches to the chakras.

You may experience sensations of awakening in your energy system as you continue your journey to increasing mastery through the brain-wave training described in this book. Should this occur, this chapter will provide you with enough fundamental information, exercises, and meditations on the chakras and kundalini energy to allow you to approach your energetic experience with the clarity and knowledge you need in order to consciously assist your awakening.

According to many different meditation systems, it is the task of the individual consciousness to raise, balance, and refine the kundalini energy force. This involves opening and balancing the chakras in a flowing harmony, throughout the total body, mind, and spirit system.

The word chakra means "wheel" in Sanskrit. The seven principle chakras in the Indian tantric tradition lie along the major channel of subtle energy, called *shushumna,* which is located along the spinal column. These vortices of energy are experienced as the points where the body and the spirit connect with and interpenetrate each other. Each person has a certain amount of energy available, and that energy should be distributed throughout the chakras. Each chakra is like a switch that turns on or opens up specific experiences within the body-mind. Stimulation of these psychic centers can initiate a change of consciousness and vice versa. This opening enables the blossoming of the individual's fullest potential and the realization of the higher self. Whether or not your kundalini is activated, and no matter what level your energy system is functioning on, feeling the energy moving in your body can be a positive and illuminating experience.

MEDITATION ON THE CHAKRAS

Sit comfortably with the spine erect yet relaxed. Imagine that you are being lifted up by the hairs at the back of the neck and gently settled back down again so that your head is balanced lightly on the top of your spine, and the vertebrae of the spine are in alignment.

Breathe easily and deeply and allow yourself to relax.

Next begin to focus on your chakras. When you are focusing on a chakra, send all of your attention there. When you inhale, breathe into that location, breathing light or the color of the chakra into that area. When you exhale, breathe away any impurities or toxins from that area, imagining them as discolored. Continue this practice until the color or light that you breathe out is the same color or light that you breathe in.

When you focus on a chakra, you may feel a kind of warmth there, or there may be a tingling, crawling, or itching sensation.

You may see images or symbols, receive information, or experience emotions connected with the different locations. If so, simply make a mental note of them so you can process them later. Continue meditating on that location for as long as you wish.

Start with the first chakra. Focus your attention and awareness there. You may want to imagine a sensation of energy, warmth, or tingling.

As you raise your attention from chakra to chakra, do so slowly, gently, and with awareness. See if you can feel the energetic connection or channel between any two chakras.

The chakras can be thought of as reaching through the body, linked along the spine by fine canals or channels. The energy of the body flows both up and down the central channel, shushumna, and the two channels to the right and left of the central channel, ida and pingala, that form a caduceus of energy, as well as in and out from the front and back of each chakra.

We will be looking at many elements of each chakra. You may wish to meditate only on certain aspects at one time rather than all of the aspects listed for each chakra.

THE CHAKRAS ARE:

1. *Mooladhara:* Moola means "root" or "base." This is the seat of kundalini, the root chakra at the base of the spine. Its actual location is in the perineum, midway between the genitals and the anus.

The element is earth.
The mantra is *Lam.*
The color is red.
The planet is Saturn.
The sense is smell.

This chakra governs basic existence, security, survival, and life force, and is associated with sexual and spiritual energy. In tantric Yoga, meditation on *mooladhara* awakens the shakti and may be considered one of the keys to spiritual liberation.

2. *Svadhisthana:* means "one's own abode." This chakra is located between the base of the spine and the navel at the level of the coccyx.

The element is water.
The mantra is *Vam.*
The color is orange.
The planet is Jupiter.
The sense is taste.

Bodily benefits are said to include the health of the blood, lymph, kidney, and bladder and the acuteness of the sense of taste. The chakra is associated with sexuality, reproduction and instinctive drives, past lives and karma, and joy. According to some tantric traditions, meditation on *svadhisthana* chakra leads to the mastery of the yogi's "enemies"—the passions of luxury, anger, greed, deception, pride, and envy. The second chakra rules the unconscious mind and illuminates the darkness of ignorance.

3. *Manipura:* "jewel city" or "city of jewels." This chakra is located just below and behind the navel, in the region of the first lumbar vertebra.

> The element is fire.
> The mantra is *Ram*.
> The color is yellow.
> The planet is Mars.
> The sense is sight.

This chakra relates to the balance of the system, meaning both physical balance and healthy metabolism. It also is associated with the control of fevers and the improvement of eyesight. It is said to govern will and achievement, willful action, vitality, energy, and manifestation in the outside world. According to some tantric traditions, meditation on *manipura* chakra gives the power of creation and destruction through the mastery of subtle energy.

4. *Anahata:* the spiritual heart. This is the heart chakra located directly behind the center of the chest, equidistant between the two nipples.

> The element is air.
> The mantra is *Yam*.
> The color is green.
> The planet is Venus.
> The sense is touch.

This is the psychic center that is said to be the root of all emotions. It is a delicate center, associated with the health of the lungs and air passages, easy bodily movements, and sensitivity of touch. It is identified with purity, creativity, and the ability to heal, where the thoughts and desires of the individual are materialized and fulfilled. It is the seat of unconditional love, love free of expectation, and divine love. According to various tantric traditions, meditation on *anahata* chakra leads to the mastery of the spoken word, the power of becoming invisible, of flying, of walking on water . . .

5. *Vishudda:* the throat chakra, also known as the "akashic center." This chakra is located inside the neck just below and behind the Adam's apple.

> The element is ether.
> The mantra is *Ham*.
> The color is blue.
> The planet is Mercury.
> The sense is hearing.

This chakra is the purification center, purifying and harmonizing opposites. It is associated with sensitivity of hearing and abundant energy, as well as higher discrimination, eloquence, communication, and self-expression. The taste of nectar is said to be experienced with this chakra's opening. This chakra is the gateway to liberation, leading beyond the physical and emotional planes into the astral spaces. Meditation on *vishudda* chakra brings the meditator to the threshold of the "great liberation" or the attainment of consciousness.

6. *Ajna:* the command center, also known as the "third eye." This chakra is located between the eyebrows at the highest point of the bridge of the nose (not in the center of the forehead).

The mantra is *Aum*.
The color is indigo.
The planets are the sun and moon.
This center is concerned with the mind, which governs all of
the senses.

It is associated with heightened intuition, clairvoyance and ESP,
insight and vision. Meditation on *ajna* chakra allows the yogi to see
no duality. Developing the ability of "single seeing," the meditator
becomes witness of the universe. (The awakening of *ajna* chakra allows the full experience of "inside/outside" that is referred to in
Chapter One.)

7. *Sahasrara:* the crown chakra located at the top of the head.

The mantra is *Aum* or *Om*.
The color is purple.
The image is of a thousand-petaled lotus opening.

This is the source of the halo that surrounds the head of spiritually evolved beings. It governs the organs and tissues of the whole
body. Tantric traditions consider this chakra to symbolize the
threshold between the psychic and spiritual realms. Meditation on
sahasrara chakra brings raised cosmic consciousness and unity with
the source or Godhead.

Now take a few moments to sit in meditation.

■　■　■

You may wish to move back down through the chakras and note
which ones feel open, full, and free flowing, and which ones
might feel like they need further meditation.

Take some time on your own now to explore your chakras in
  meditation.

■ ■ ■

*As a closure for this meditation, I suggest you take a large, blank
piece of paper and crayons, markers, or colored pencils and draw
your chakra system as you experienced it during the meditation. Each
time you practice this meditation, you may wish to make a new drawing, noting the changes that occur in your energy and the progression
that develops as you open your chakras.*

A PERSONAL STORY

The basis for most of the chakra information in this chapter is Indian and
tantric in nature. My original tantric teacher, Swami Satyananda Saraswati
of the Bihar School of Yoga in Bihar, India, provided me with the primary
structure for my knowledge of chakras. Swami Satyananda had an active
ashram in London and was a frequent visitor there. After I moved back
to Boulder, Colorado, in the 1980s, two of his top disciples, Swami
Vivekananda from Australia and Swami Amritananda from Bihar, came
to visit me on separate occasions and hold extended **darshan** (a kind of
spiritual meeting) at my center there.

I felt particularly connected with Swami Amritananda, as she was a
woman a few years younger than me who had been raised by Swami
Satyananda since the age of three to carry on his work. I was eight
months pregnant with my son at the time of her visit, and she was especially respectful of my unborn child and me. She performed rituals and
blessings for the upcoming birth that were particularly deep and meaningful to me. Her entourage, the dozen or so followers and assistants that
she brought with her, were significantly impressed when she went into a
trance and blessed and named my unborn son "Yogendra." They re-

spectfully and carefully explained to me that that means, "He who is master of himself and king of the gods." What a beginning!

Swami Satyananda states in his book, *Kundalini Tantra,* "Whatever happens in spiritual life, it is related to the awakening of kundalini. And the goal of every form of spiritual life, whether you call it samadhi, nirvana, moksha, communion, union, kaivalya, liberation or whatever, is in fact awakening of kundalini." His books provide a systematic and complex practice aimed at awakening each chakra in turn to facilitate the complete awakening of kundalini.

THE BRAIN WAVES OF KUNDALINI

I have had the opportunity to measure several Westerners who were undergoing what they identified as a kundalini awakening. They all had some combination of experiences that have been referred to in this chapter as various "symptoms" of kundalini awakening. A number of individuals have come to me over the years in fear or uncertainty about the experiences they were having. Almost every individual having a kundalini awakening that I have had the opportunity to measure on the Mind Mirror has exhibited some form of the awakened mind. They were by no means all stabilized, organized, and complete awakened minds; however, they each showed the characteristics of beta, alpha, theta, and delta in a relationship that began to enable the flow of information between the unconscious, subconscious, and conscious minds. They were awakening.

THE CIRCULATION OF CHI

Oriental meditation systems such as Chi Kung (sometimes spelled "Qi Gong") also relate directly to the energy system as we have already seen, usually using the word *"chi"* or *"qi"* to mean energy. The Oriental methods of energy movement are often more con-

cerned with the *circulation* of energy within the body and the con-
servation, maintenance, and building of that energy, rather than the
more linear progression of the energy resulting in tapping a higher
energy source found in the Indian traditions.

In a general way of looking at it, the Indian or Hindu systems
are more focused on afterlife, reincarnation, and spiritual evolution
and are not as concerned with the health of the body here and now.
These practices tend to take the focus of the energy out of the body
and use it to reach a higher plane of awareness, peacefulness, and
bliss. The Chinese energy meditation systems, on the other hand,
tend to focus more specifically in the body to maintain a greater
awareness of the life-enhancing and health benefits that the energy
system has for the body right here and now, in this incarnation.

Both have much merit. My own early history is more in the tantric
and Indian traditions, primarily seeking higher spiritual awareness.
However, as a result of bodily injury, I later connected very strongly
with some of the Oriental traditions. I now find great benefit in the
Oriental circulation of energy as well. Meditation in this way can also
be useful in *slowing down and grounding* the awakening of the linear
progression of energy up through the chakras from the root to the
crown, if you find your kundalini process out of control.

THE CHI MUST HAVE INTENTION

Another Chi Kung master I have worked with, this time in San
Francisco, is Master Bingkun Hu, Ph.D. Master Hu, although Chinese, now leads workshops on the West Coast of California. He
teaches, "*Chi* without intention is empty and ineffective. Allow your
chi to have the intention of strength, health, fullness, and balance."

> "Allow your *chi* to have the intention of strength,
> health, fullness, and balance."

THE ORBIT

In the Chinese practice of Chi Kung, the energy, or chi, *is circulated through the body in what is known as the "microcosmic orbit." There are at least four major forms of the orbit depending on the practice you are learning. Below is the most basic form.*

Either sit upright on the edge of a chair with your feet flat on the ground, your knees at right angles, and your spine erect with your back not touching the back of the chair; or sit cross-legged in a full or half "lotus" position on the floor. Sitting on the edge of a stiff pillow such as a *zafu* will help by raising your tailbone and lowering your knees, thus relieving pressure from the joints in your legs.

Begin by focusing on the area just below and behind your navel, called the "hara."

Let your mind clear, and allow the energy to build there.

When you are ready, on your exhalation, take your awareness and the energy down to the root chakra in the perineum.

On your inhalation, draw the energy up your spine in the back to the crown of your head.

Linger there for a few moments . . .

Then exhale and draw the energy down your front, back to the root chakra.

Connect this energy circuit by touching the tip of your tongue to the roof of your mouth, either just behind the root of your teeth or just behind the "bump" in the roof of your mouth. This allows the energy to flow smoothly down through your facial area where the link is often broken at the mouth. (Remember to keep the back of your tongue relaxed at the same time.)

The circulation of energy forms an oval or orbit from the top of your head to your perineum, moving up the back and down the front. Move up on inhalation and down on exhalation.

If you cannot move your awareness and the energy all the way up the spine in one breath, allow yourself several breaths to draw it up.

On the inhalation, draw it up; on the exhalation, let it rest where it is. On the downward flow, draw it down on the exhalation, letting it rest on the inhalation.

Breaths can be counted to aid in focus and concentration. Count in groups of ten—one count for each complete orbit. Each group of ten is called a "round." You may wish to begin this exercise with three rounds or thirty breaths.

A contrasting style of meditation is the more linear form of energetic awakening that allows you to go "Up and Out." This meditation is much more in keeping with the Hindu, Indian, and tantric styles, which are involved not with the circulation, storage, and build-up of *chi,* as are the Oriental forms, but rather with using the energy as a transportation modality to reach a higher state of consciousness or spiritual awareness.

UP AND OUT

Sit in the same position as you did for the Orbit meditation.

Allow your mind to clear, and focus your attention on your
    perineum at the root of your spine. Let the energy build there.

When the energy feels strong, and you are ready, draw your
    awareness and the energy up your spine when you inhale.
Bring it all the way up to the top of your head.

You can do this in one breath, or you can choose to use several breaths and take it slowly, chakra by chakra. Bring the energy straight up through the center of your chakras (the shushumna *channel) to the crown.*

Rest in the crown chakra on the exhalation.

On the next inhalation, ride the energy out into the universe . . .

And connect with your higher self . . .
and your divine source . . .

■ ■ ■

When you are ready to return,
slowly allow yourself to come back down to your crown chakra . . .
down through the top of your head,
down through the central channel of your energy system . . .
to the root chakra.

Rest in the root chakra for a few minutes before you close your
    meditation.

Kundalini Meditation

These meditations are not designed to specifically stimulate kundalini, simply to familiarize you with your energy system. In the
course of practicing any meditation, whether in this book or not, if
you should become uncomfortable with any of the symptoms described in this chapter, you may wish to stop and return to this type
of meditation later.

Many people are not affected by the awakening of kundalini
with noticeable symptoms. The movement of energy, however, is often a common and expected phenomenon when practicing meditation. This may take the form of having *more* energy to expend,
feeling more rested and in need of less sleep, and feeling more alert
and alive, ready to fully participate in life.

After meditation, sensory input often becomes stronger and
more vivid. Colors are brighter, the senses of taste and smell are
heightened, and there is a perception of clarity previously lack-
ing. On completing a meditation, when you reopen your eyes,
try looking at everything as if it were new, as if you were seeing it
for the first time. Allow yourself to carry the benefit of the state

you have been experiencing with you back into your active, everyday life.

KUNDALINI MEDITATION
With thanks to C. Maxwell Cade

Sit comfortably with your spine straight, and allow your eyes to close.

Allow yourself to take a few minutes to clear your mind and
   relax . . .

Begin to experience yourself going into a very deep state of
   meditation—
It's almost a sense of falling backward . . .
Backward into softness . . .
Backward into warmth . . .
Backward into yourself . . .

Falling . . .
Experience yourself at first as floating down . . .
Then as drifting down . . .
Then falling faster and faster . . .
Down through dark, seemingly infinite spaces.
Falling farther and farther and having sensations of falling that will
   carry you very deeply into meditation . . .
And the farther you fall, the deeper you seem to go . . .

And now, you will find that you are still falling,
But falling more slowly
As you near the most profound depths
Within this *circular* space
Where you are going to settle softly and easily
Down upon a substance able to support you,
Here, in the *cylindrical* depths of your meditation.

And you will find yourself becoming aware, gradually at first,
Of rays of white light reaching down to you,
Sparkling white light . . .
A cone of light surrounding you now,
Growing brighter and brighter,
Sparkling and shimmering, warming you with its radiance.
It washes over you, suffusing your whole body,
Changing in appearance from one moment to the next,
But always brilliantly white, cascading around you,
And sometimes appearing to you now as a white and golden light.

A wondrously beautiful white and golden light,
Dazzling . . . unearthly . . .
All around you as your body moves into it . . .
And feeling your body become much taller,
And a feeling of more and more elongation . . .
The body becoming taller, slimmer . . .
And this bringing with it what you are experiencing now as an
    indescribable but strongly spiritual feeling . . .
Something more than human that your body is feeling as you stand
    there so tall, elongated . . .
With the dazzling white and golden light all around you,
And so much a part of you that your body now seems to you more a
    body of light than of flesh.

And that light continues glowing brighter and brighter
As you feel yourself to be merging into the light,
Becoming the light,
And finding your awareness now to be of yourself as a shower of
    sparks descending,
Descending to become a pool of white light,
There on the ground where your awareness is, where you are,
And you *are* a pool of white light—
Pool of energies about to be unleashed.

Energies, forces gathering there,
And that white light now leaping upward,
Soaring upward,
A column of white and golden fire
Reaching up, and up, and up,
Through that almost endlessly long cylindrical space,
A column of white and golden flame that you are a part of,
And you have no awareness beyond that column of white and
    golden fire.

A column that is glowing whiter and whiter,
A column of white fire that you are a part of,
Reaching upward from the very center of the earth,
Surging, flowing upward and upward,
And finally bursting out through the opening at the earth's
    surface,
And still surging upward, far, far up into the skies.

A pillar of white light
Rising from the earth's center,
And soaring outward endlessly into the black vastness of
    space,
As if its power would allow it to penetrate the universe.
And knowing the feeling of awesome power,
Of sublime beauty, and wonder, and energy,
As you partake of that column of white fire.

Feeling yourself now sinking backward with it,
Back and down,
Back and down again,
Back past the earth's surface,
Back and down the cylinder
Until down at the bottom, only a small white flame is burning.

And you rise out of that fire,
And the fire is extinguished.

■　■　■

And now going even deeper . . .
And allowing yourself to go deeper and deeper . . .
and finding yourself here in this place
but having access to some very potent energies within you . . .

And focus your consciousness now on the base of your spine . . .
Becoming aware of a pool of gently swirling but potentially
    extremely powerful energy there.
Wholly focused on the base of your spine,
On that pool of tremendous energies . . .

And you may experience at first a kind of tingling or warmth
and increasingly stronger sensations
as you direct that energy to rise up along your spine.

Draw the energy now up from the root chakra . . .

Through the second chakra at the top of the pubic bone . . .

Up through the navel . . .

And up through the heart . . .

Up through the throat . . .

Through the third eye between the eyebrows . . .

And all the way up to the crown at the top of the head . . .

Draw the energy out through the crown chakra . . .

Up and out . . .
up and out . . .
out into the universe . . .

A beam of light
reaching high, high up into the sky.

Allow yourself to ride that beam of light
out as far as you wish to go,

And allow yourself
to have a vision . . .

And to meditate . . .

■ ■ ■

And back
and down . . .

And back . . .
and down . . .

And back and down
the column of light . . .
And back and down through the crown chakra,
down through the third eye,
down through the throat,
down through the heart,
down through the navel,
down through the second chakra,
down to the root chakra . . .

Where only a small flame is burning,
and that fire is extinguished.

Take a few moments now to simply sit . . .
and to meditate . . .

And just notice what you are experiencing . . .

Allow yourself to find an image, a word, a body sensation, a landmark
that describes your experience of this meditation . . .
and take a few moments
to prepare yourself
for closure . . .

And in your own time,
when you are ready,
allow yourself to complete your meditation,
and reawaken
back in the outside space
feeling alert, refreshed, and full of energy.

*You may wish to verbalize, write, or draw your experience in order
to fully ground it in your conscious mind.*

DEVELOPING THE
QUALITIES OF MASTERY

The Fine Points of Awakening Your Mind

For almost three decades, I have had the opportunity to witness the brain waves of many people with awakened minds. These observations and interactions allowed me to understand what is really involved in mastery. Having beta, alpha, theta, and delta at the same time does not automatically make you a master. As I stated at the beginning of this book, I have identified a number of characteristics or qualities that are included in the contents of the state of mastery. Along with these positive qualities, you can find an endless variety of additional creative and spiritual abilities.

Mastery can be found in the flower arranger engrossed in her creative art, the CEO negotiating in the boardroom, the psychotherapist helping a client in crisis, the healer easing pain, the finely trained athlete performing his sport, the actor delivering a perfect scene, the engineer creating a new design, the musician composing, the meditator in samadhi, the spiritual teacher simply being. . . . The number of possibilities is infinite.

This chapter will investigate more deeply the fine points of awakening your mind and mastering the power of your brain waves, from challenges you might encounter as you begin relating to the outside world with these new brain-wave states to a deeper look at the development of the positive qualities of mastery. In the end, it is important to understand that we must demonstrate both the state and the content of higher consciousness to embody true mastery.

Changing our brain waves and awakening is, in a sense, like changing the lens through which we view our reality. Whatever object we focus our attention on can be experienced in a different way if we use our mastery techniques. Whole new vistas emerge as we look at "problems" from more aware or diverse levels. These new perspectives may open doors of untapped creativity, offering ideas we would not have developed from a "beta-only" mind. They may help us change directions to a more appropriate or productive course of action. Or they may help us stay the course at a time when we otherwise would have conceded defeat or at least opted for a less challenging and rewarding alternative.

However, you may also find having an awakened mind in itself is a challenging experience at times. Both internally and externally, being aware of more, seeing beyond your beta, both down in the depths within and as you relate to the outside world, can be formidable if not downright difficult at times.

One of the things that can help create the most difficulty from an awakened mind is seeing with awareness whatever *is* but not yet being able to ascertain the best course of action from that sight. Another difficulty is seeing what is and knowing what needs to happen but not yet having the perseverance or perhaps ability to make it happen. And finally there is seeing what is, knowing what needs to happen, feeling that you have the ability to make it happen, but being unable to convince others of the correct action or show them how to have that vision, therefore feeling thwarted and/or isolated in your progress.

All three of the above possibilities can be frustrating at best and even disheartening. There may indeed be times when you wonder why you ever wanted to start down the road of personal awareness.

Wouldn't it be better to just lumber along in the darkness, staying comfortable in the bliss of ignorance?

Certainly yes at times, it would *feel* better to imagine that we could close the door on personal growth and awakening, especially when the path is rocky or the truths are painful. But the rewards of emotional and spiritual evolution far outweigh those difficult times in the long run.

We are on a path of personal evolution and learning mastery. It may take us many years, decades, or even lifetimes, but nevertheless, we are being drawn inexorably toward our own personal spiritual best. We can slow this journey down, but we cannot stop it. Nor would we really want to, ultimately—to spend the rest of eternity in darkness or mediocrity is contrary to the laws of human nature. This quest for evolutionary progress is inherent within our very being.

We can honor the search for excellence, high performance, and mastery not only by recognizing its rewards, but also by acknowledging its difficulties. Let's look in greater depth at these three challenges that can occur in the process of awakening.

ONLY A GLIMPSE OF AWAKENING

The first category stimulates perhaps the most frustration and greatest sense of impotence—that is, when you can see the situation clearly in the present moment but are unable to understand what to do about it or how to proceed from here. This is only partial mastery and stems from the awakening of insight and awareness—probably through the development of alpha, theta, and delta—but only in a kind of snapshot form.

You receive a glimpse of "ah-ha" enough to understand the situation, but it is a *passive* understanding. Without continuity, you won't have mastered movement through time or the ability to know how to take action on your insight.

Considering that the insight itself tends to come from the

depths of theta, and alpha gives us the imagery and sensory modality to translate it into a form understandable by our conscious minds, what may be the best action for you in this situation is to continue to practice adding beta to your meditation state. Remember, beta is the logical, conscious processing function of thought. When added to the insights of the lower frequencies, it can give a greater ability for and understanding of the manifestation of those insights. Refer back to Chapter Five on adding the beta back, and practice those exercises if you feel stuck in this way.

Awakening without the Ability for Action

Category two is very similar to the first one but a little bit more evolved. Here you see what action needs to be done but somehow can't muster the commitment, perseverance, attitude, or conduct necessary for the accomplishment.

In both of these situations, steadfastness, persistence, and continued work on your own mastery and creative abilities will help you eventually move forward. In this situation, it might benefit you to find out more about why it is difficult for you to move forward once the course of action has become clear to you. Perhaps you might look at how staying where you are rather than progressing is serving you—in other words, the positive purpose of staying stuck. Meditations such as Healing the Block in Chapter Seven can certainly help to move you forward. You would see the block as that which is getting in the way of allowing you to complete your desired task.

Ability for Action Without Cooperation of Others

The final challenge I have outlined is perhaps the most persistent and will continue to be with you for as long as you continue your journey of finding mastery at the same time as living and functioning in the "normal" twenty-first-century world. It doesn't, however, need to continue to be a personal difficulty or an obstacle to your own growth and awakening.

The challenge I am talking about here is that of *knowing for certain* in your own mind that a particular viewpoint and course of action is, without a doubt, correct; and yet, others around you with whom you work, live, and interact are unable, at least at the beginning, to view things in the same way.

There is always a possibility that they too have an awakened insight that draws them in a different direction, a direction that is correct for them. Then it will be necessary for the two of you to either open real communication and develop an awakened approach that works for both of you in combination or agree to go your separate ways on that particular issue. However, if the other person or people are also practicing mastery and awakening, that is not the real difficulty that I am referring to here.

I'm talking about truly *seeing and knowing with all of your heart and deepest intuitive powers* a truth or path of right action but being unable to convince those around you of the validity of that vision or the necessity of those actions. This can be compounded by even seeing the course that will occur over the coming time line that will involve either:

a. their gradual acceptance and understanding of the picture and therefore eventual movement into right action, or

b. their continued inability to grasp the right action, resulting in the deterioration or loss of progress on this path.

In either case, your task is to remain true to yourself and true to right action while at the same time continuing your journey of awakening and mastery. Sometimes it is necessary to just sit back, relax, and realize that you have to wait for others to catch up. At other times, some wisely placed actions to control damage may help to ease the situation. Obviously, the more autonomy you have in your job and indeed in your life, the more you will be able to alleviate such situations.

> As always, nonjudgmental generosity of spirit and acceptance of the other individuals for the beautiful beings that they are is also intrinsic to mastery.

Once you've tried your best, if you really can't make what you *think* you know to be the proper course of action happen, then perhaps it's best to back off and stop worrying about it. It may just not be the right time for that eventuality. Or perhaps the people you are in conflict with know something that you don't know, or are truly needing *for their own evolution* to experience the course they have laid out that you disagree with.

The Tao can be, at times, an unfathomable thing and may have an entirely different plan. There also may be unforeseen or unknowable factors at play that even the most awakened of people could not have anticipated. Your job also is to *trust* in your own process of awakening and to *trust* the Tao well enough to be able to flow through a difficult situation so that you can continue to move forward to the next step on your path.

EGO

Another major stumbling block for some people after awakening has actually begun is difficulty in dealing with the fact that this is happening to *them*. They take it personally, and they may begin to see themselves as "better" than others or "more evolved." As soon as this kind of personal ownership sets in, the individual is headed for trouble. Neither the awakening of the mind nor the awakening of the energy system progresses in the face of this kind of possessiveness. The ego itself provides a block that the inner being must work through in order to move forward. The more the ego tries to hold on to and build its inflation, the harder the higher self has to work to do its job of awakening. The unfortunate result of this conflict may be the individual who proudly proclaims, "My ego is smaller than yours!"

SELF-ESTEEM PENDULUM

Whenever anyone deals with an "ego problem," it is an issue of self-esteem. I see self-esteem problems as being on a pendulum. At one end of the pendulum is an over-inflated ego, and at the other end is low self-esteem. Usually when you have one problem, the other is lurking nearby. All it takes is a simple swing of the pendulum for you to be experiencing the extreme opposite.

Many people think that the solution to this swing between ego extremes is to find a nice safe balance in the middle. Absolutely not! The only real solution is to *get off the pendulum altogether!* Trying to find that balance is still battling with the polarity pulls of both extremes, even if the balance is found and maintained for an extended period of time. The threat is always there for the scales to tip and the pendulum to swing to one end or the other, or both in quick succession, which is often the case.

So how does an individual get off the ego pendulum? Detachment and letting go are the main answers. But they are easy words to say and often difficult concepts to comprehend in this situation. The easiest and most direct route off the pendulum is to accept that there is a power greater than yourself that is ultimately in charge of everything and that *you are not in control.* You did not cause the awakening.

This is not a religious book. However, when we talk about awakening, we cannot avoid *spirituality.* It doesn't matter what you call that power, it only matters that you do not see yourself as the highest authority. If you see yourself as the highest authority, you are headed for a fall, and the block in your awakening could be much longer as a result. The more faith you have in some divine order in the universe—whether your higher power is God with a capital G, nature, source, Buddha, Jesus, love, light, or *any other way of understanding a power greater than yourself*—the easier it will be for you to let go of your own ego.

DEVELOPING THE QUALITIES OF MASTERY

It is valuable to develop certain qualities and characteristics that will serve you, not only with the kinds of difficulties mentioned in this chapter, but in all major areas of your life. Let us return for a deeper look at the qualities mentioned at the beginning of this book.

QUALITIES OF MASTERY

Compassion

Detachment

Nonjudgment

Clarity

Equanimity

Service

Love

Does it seem like a tall order? If you expect yourself to have fully mastered and integrated all of these characteristics at once, NOW, then it *is* an impossibly tall order. There is danger in seeing this as so impossibly idealistic that you discount it and back away from even trying to begin the development of these qualities. Understanding and practicing the following principles will help you overcome this danger.

First of all, you have to have these qualities for yourself. Before you can expect yourself to genuinely and authentically have these attitudes toward others outside of you, turn this attention, awareness, and generosity inward. Only when you can love and feel compassion toward yourself can you truly feel it for another.

Secondly, small amounts are better than none at all. You will develop these qualities in layers. People rarely wake up finding that overnight they have become compassionate, detached, nonjudgmental, etc. It may even happen so gradually that neither you nor those close to you are aware of a change occurring. However, as you become more and more comfortable with the internal experience of these characteristics, there will eventually be a point of no return, a time when you are more comfortable being compassionate than not being compassionate.

And finally, don't expect these qualities to be permanent. As you develop the layers of these qualities, they will come and go with greater and lesser intensity depending on the external situation and your internal condition. At times, you may feel you have some or all of these qualities quite finely developed, only to find the opposite staring you in the face. You may find yourself asking yourself, "Where is all that judgment coming from?" And the answer may be glaringly apparent or firmly hidden from view.

Acknowledge yourself for little things. Recognize that at least you became *aware* of the judgment and did not continue it totally unconsciously, even if you are having difficulty stopping it.

Let's take a closer look at these qualities:

Compassion: The concept of compassion has two components: understanding and empathy toward your own or another person's difficulty, and an attitude or action designed to help. It involves a desire to help alleviate suffering.

Detachment: Detachment, on the other hand, means not allowing yourself to be unduly influenced, imbalanced, or negatively affected by the actions of another. It involves the understanding that we cannot force change on other people. We give them the freedom to do their best and give ourselves the freedom from holding on to them and trying to control them. Detachment in relationship to the self is about letting go of the need to force your own perfection—detaching from the foibles, imperfections, and peculiarities of your innate human personality. You can read this both as letting go of these frailties or perceived weaknesses and as letting go of judging these perceived weaknesses and just allowing them to be.

Nonjudgment: The judgment we are talking about letting go of involves criticism and condemnation. Becoming nonjudgmental is vital to the process of mastery, awakening, and self-development. *This does not, however, mean losing discernment,* which can be defined more as insight, understanding, and making wise choices. It eliminates the elements of reproach and blame, leaving the idea of keen perception.

Clarity: Similar to keen perception, having clarity means having understanding and certainty. However, it also means presenting yourself to yourself and others in an understandable and not confused or confusing way. Being clear, by its reference to "easy to see" (clear day) and "easy to see through" (clear glass) can also imply a sense of translucence, or of brightness and lusterousness or even light, that, in a spiritual context, means an awareness of a higher spiritual state. When you are free of the murky darkness of the repressed "stuff" of the subconscious, you are clear or have clarity.

Equanimity: Equanimity is similar to balance in that it relates to a kind of self-possession, self-assurance, and presence of mind that brings calmness, peacefulness, and tranquility. It allows us to have an even temper, composure, and poise in a difficult situation.

Service: By its very nature, mastery implies that the master is aware of his or her life's work or purpose on the planet. Someone who is spiritually and emotionally aware of their very reason for being knows that their life's work intrinsically involves some aspect of helping others on the planet, being of service, regardless of the modality chosen or the people worked with. It is even possible to be of service by simply *being* in a state of awakening or God-consciousness and drawing that positive and constructive energy into the world and those around you.

Love: The capacity for love is crucial for awakening and mastery. This tender, warm feeling mixed with joy and deep affection may be focused on one individual or on humanity in general and, as awakening continues, on a deep, heartfelt devotion to God or divine consciousness. Again, the flow is in all directions. It is as important to be able to receive love as to give love; and it is vital to love the self as well. How could we possibly expect someone else to love us if we don't love ourselves? Indeed, love is perhaps the single most vital quality to nurture in yourself as you find your way down your path of awakening.

And with that, I will bring to a close talking *about* the qualities of mastery and offer you a meditation that can help you begin to experience and develop these qualities within yourself. Developing these qualities will help you face and deal with *any* of the challenges that are likely to meet you as you continue on your path toward mastery.

THE QUALITIES OF MASTERY

Take a few minutes to settle yourself and prepare yourself in the
usual way for meditation.

Let go of any particular expectations
and allow yourself to become very present,

right here,
right now . . .

Allow your mind to clear of all thoughts,
and focus on your breathing.
Breathing easily and deeply . . .
breathing relaxation into your body,
and breathing away any tension.
Breathing relaxation into your mind,
and breathing away any remaining thoughts . . .
. . . and relax . . .

Scan through your body to make sure that the *whole* of your body is
    relaxed.
Relaxing your head, and the muscles of your face . . .
. . . paying particular attention to your lips, tongue, throat, and
    jaws.
Relaxing your neck and shoulders . . .
Allow the relaxation to flow down your arms all the way to your
    fingertips.

Allow waves of relaxation to flow into your chest and upper back . . .
Flowing down your spine and deep into your stomach . . .
right into the very center of your body . . .
the very center of your being.

Allow the relaxation to flow through your hips and pelvis
and down both legs . . .
all the way to your feet and toes . . .

So that your whole body is relaxed . . .

Your mind is quiet and still . . .
very still . . .

Your emotions are calm and clear . . .

Your spirit is peaceful . . .

Your body, mind, emotions, and spirit
are in harmony . . .

■ ■ ■

Now allow yourself to begin to go even deeper inside . . .
right down to the very center . . .
to the very depth . . .
of your innermost being . . .

Remember your landmarks for your deepest meditation . . .
and re-create those sensory experiences inside yourself . . .

It may almost be a sense of falling . . .
dropping . . .
gently . . .
slowly . . .
down . . .
inside . . .

You may have body sensations of expansion . . .
growing . . .
pulsation . . .
even throbbing.
Or you may lose all sense of your body boundaries . . .
as you continue
going down . . .

You may see visions . . .
lights . . .

colors . . .
deep blues and purples . . .
indigo . . .
and violet . . .

You may hear sounds . . .
music . . .
even voices . . .
as you continue moving down . . .
inside . . .

. . . until you reach the experience . . .
. . . of peace . . .

■   ■   ■

And from this place of deep peace and relaxation within
    yourself,
you can now begin to imagine or create
some images in your mind.

Allow yourself to sensualize a large stage inside a theater.

You are in the audience of this empty theater . . .
in one of the first few rows.
You can feel the seat you are sitting in . . .
see the colors of the open curtain.

You are aware of the height of the ceiling
and the expansiveness of the room.
Even though it is only dimly lit,
you can see clearly and easily around you
with your sense of knowing.

You feel safe, secure, and expectant . . .
knowing something important is going to happen.

There is a spotlight shining on the left-hand side of the stage,
and in the middle of this round circle of light,
you see yourself . . .

Illuminated by the light,
but still
just you,
your ordinary, everyday self,
With all your foibles, insecurities, limitations, and peculiarities . . .
and with all your individuality and beauty.

Notice what you are wearing . . .
how you are standing . . .
the expression on your face . . .
your body language and movements . . .

Just for a moment
enter that body
and experience it from the inside . . .
standing on the stage,
looking out at yourself seated in the audience.

Notice how you feel . . .

Now go back and reenter the observer, the you that is seated in the
    audience . . .
and look again at your ordinary self
standing on the stage.
Notice any changes that have occurred . . .
Or anything new you have become aware of that you didn't see
    before . . .

Slowly, the spotlight fades on the left-hand side of the stage.
And as that light goes down,
a light goes up on the right-hand side of the stage.
In this spotlight, there is another version of you standing . . .
This is the you that is going to embody the qualities of
    mastery.

As you watch, you see—with a clear sense of knowing—this
    person . . .
this version of you . . .
standing,
calmly . . .
peacefully . . .
waiting . . .

And very slowly,
you are going to begin to give him or her
the qualities of mastery you know are possible.

First, just see them from the outside.

Begin by seeing this individual have the quality of
    compassion.
Perhaps it has to do with the expression on the face,
or the position they are standing in . . .
or perhaps it's just a sense of knowing
that the "you" that is standing there in the spotlight
has the quality of compassion.

Now, also begin to give them the quality of detachment.

Allow them to be nonjudgmental.

You can also see in them a kind of clarity.

Add to this the sense of equanimity, of being truly balanced within
   themselves.

Now add to this the certainty that they are in service.

And finally . . .
add love . . .
the sense that this person you are looking at is radiating . . .
infused with . . .
surrounded by . . .
and emanating . . .
love . . .

■   ■   ■

All of these qualities,
present and available,
active,
in this "you" that you see upon the stage.

Perhaps you see it in the face,
the expression . . .
perhaps you see it in the body,
the stance,
the radiation of energy . . .

Perhaps you perceive it in the tone of voice
or some other indescribable quality
of being
that you can see or sense in yourself,
standing there
so calm and composed
on the stage.

And now,
allow yourself to
enter this body
and experience it from the inside . . .
standing on the stage
looking out at yourself seated in the audience.

Notice what it feels like . . .
to stand there so tall,
calm,
and composed . . .

What it feels like
to experience
compassion . . .

detachment . . .

nonjudgment . . .

clarity . . .

equanimity . . .

service . . .

love . . .

■   ■   ■

What you do now is up to you.
You may want to enter and remain with one of your three
   selves.

You may want to merge all three of them to become one
    "you." . . .

Embodying the qualities of mastery . . .

Allow yourself to find the completion that feels right for you.

■   ■   ■

In a little while,
you are going to begin to bring your meditation
to a close . . .

Before you do,
take some time to be aware
of what you have learned
from this meditation . . .

What can you bring back with you from this experience?
What landmarks can you find to help you return to this state
in the future?

Use images, colors, sounds, body sensations, words . . .
anything that will help you mark
and master
the embodiment of these qualities.

■   ■   ■

And return in the usual way whenever you are ready.

MEDITATION AND AWAKENING

A Bigger Picture

O nce you have read this book, what is the practical reality that awaits you? Developing an awakened mind requires personal commitment. People who wish to achieve this goal have learned to integrate tools for brain-wave mastery into their lives, creating a meditation routine that is both enjoyable and tailored for their individual needs.

Once someone has found his or her rhythm with meditation and has developed a regular practice, long-term effects may begin to take place. These effects vary greatly and depend upon the individual. Some results come quickly, others may take time to mature.

Among these long-term effects, you may find greater skill in handling unexpected situations; more mental flexibility and increased creativity; greater intuition and insight; fewer health problems, or a better ability to deal with the health problems that do occur; increased emotional stability; less overall stress; and a heightened spiritual awareness.

If you meditate regularly, you will almost certainly feel changes. These changes can be as subtle as a gentle sense of relaxation or serenity, or they might manifest dramatically as periods of ecstasy and bliss. You may also experience mood swings or feelings of confusion or sadness as you undertake the house cleaning of your subconscious. With practice, you will learn how to use even the downtimes beneficially. Your dreams may also change, as well as the quality and quantity of your sleep.

The timing of the effects of meditation is different for everyone. If you hit a low period, bear in mind that all of the changes are ultimately leading toward the positive—toward the development of your mind and the evolution of your being. If there are some dark rooms inside to clean out, or you discover personal changes that you need to make, welcome these as opportunities to further your journey.

The brain-wave development and meditation training that I have described draws upon many resources and uses a myriad of techniques. You can use these meditations on their own or in combination with other practices that you may already be familiar with.

EAST MEETS WEST— MEDITATIONS ON CONTENT VERSUS STATE

In my work with students of Zen or those who have focused almost primarily on the "mindfulness" type of meditation, I have encountered a recurring question. Why meditate with content if your sole purpose for meditation is one of enlightenment?

The most obvious brain-wave based answer may sometimes satisfy them. The brain waves of the awakened mind are much easier to develop when content is integrated into the state training. For example, developing theta can be much easier by *using* the content of the subconscious to access it first. This integrated approach of using content to help with the access of state and using state to help with the access of content forms the basis of my approach to *Awakening the Mind*.

However, this answer is sometimes not sufficient for long-term

Zen meditators who have spent many years practicing mindfulness. They often already have an awakened or near-awakened mind brainwave state developed from their years of practice, but somehow they still do not have the content or personal inner experience of mastery of a true awakened mind. They want to know what is going on.

The answer is quite simple. Typical Zen or mindfulness meditation is a *preparation* for awakening. This style of meditation serves to begin to, or even fully, prepare the mind for enlightenment. But no matter how long it is practiced, **it does not facilitate the attainment of enlightenment in even the most prepared mind.** Zen meditators may have spent years withdrawing and trying to learn to turn *off* beta, while what they need to do is learn to turn *on* the experience of the awakened mind.

In the Zen tradition, enlightenment comes in a flash, a moment of intense insight from some seemingly innocuous or random event. It does not come directly from practice.

Zen and other Buddhist traditions do have content-based meditation, often called **contemplation**. It is during the contemplation of some object, concept, or event that one may experience this flash of true spiritual awakening—hence the usage of the Zen **koan**. The purpose of the many years of mindfulness practice is to train the meditator to be able to concentrate with the correct state on the content of contemplation, thereby being ready for that moment of grace when awakening strikes.

Probably the most familiar of the Zen koans to the Westerner is, "What is the sound of one hand clapping?" Koan, or *kong an,* means literally "a public case" in Japanese—a description of a scenario in which a master dialogues with a student asking a (sometimes even innocuous) question that is unanswerable with only beta brain waves. Seen sometimes as a form of challenge, the essence of the koan can often be reduced to one question, but it is also frequently presented in the form of a verse. In pondering the paradox of the koan, the adept student may access an understanding or knowledge that transcends thought and facilitates awakening. This is not an "empty mind" meditation. Indeed, to the contrary, it is the contemplation of specific content by the practitioner with a properly prepared state of mind that brings the flash of enlightenment.

> At high noon
> Or in the dark moonless night there is a light.
> Can you see it?
> And, by the way, who are you?
> MICHAEL WENGER, *33 Fingers,* Clear Glass Publishing, San Francisco, 1974

BRAIN-WAVE TRAINING ENHANCES
ANY FORM OF MEDITATION

There are many forms of traditional meditation that provide wonderful spiritual tools. It is important to understand that working with the state and the content of consciousness through brain-wave development does not need to conflict with other forms of meditation. Rather, the brain-wave training will enhance other practices even more by updating them with our current scientific knowledge and research and by maximizing the meditator's own resources.

When people come to me who have spent many years and invested much energy in the traditional pursuit of Zen meditation, they usually have one of two reactions to this brain-wave information. They may grasp instantly the concepts that I am presenting and become interested students of this new approach, integrating it into their own format quickly and easily. Or, they may argue that an empty mind is the only way.

The strong majority of the spiritual masters or those who are already awakened whom I have explained my work to tend to be interested, accepting, and excited, not only by the general possibilities that it presents, but also by the specific implications it may have for their particular work. Often, the unfulfilled seekers can have the greatest resistance to the idea of integrating science within their meditation. Some who have devoted a large amount of time to their practice, without return, have occasionally had trouble finding that if they just did it a little differently, it might be much more effective.

> The principles and work in *Awakening the Mind* can be applied to any practice, spiritual approach, or religious philosophy or technique without undermining or diminishing the specific characteristics and power of that modality. This work may be used by anyone to enhance his or her own practice, or it may be used as a stand-alone philosophy in and of itself without the need for another spiritual format.

"BEYOND ENLIGHTENMENT"

What do the masters do when they themselves want to go higher?

C. Maxwell Cade, my original master, who discovered the awakened mind brain-wave pattern, used to enjoy hooking people up to his early-version Mind Mirror EEG, walking around behind them out of sight, and standing there until they produced an awakened mind. It was his version of *Shakti-pat,* or "the transmission of power." It rarely took longer than a few minutes for the desired state to appear. When he saw the awakened mind pattern appear on the Mind Mirror, he would smile, nod his head, whisper "very good" under his breath, and move on.

My dear friend Geoffrey Blundell, the British master engineer who developed the Mind Mirror EEG as part of his quest for consciousness understanding, has long been a Tibetan Buddhist. Reflecting on the state of Zen awakening, he observes, "The object is to find your own true being and the face you had before you were born." Geoffrey's Tibetan master, Chogyal Namkhai Norbu (translated as "Jewel in the Sky"), teaches that the ultimate goal is to achieve "the primordial state of non-dual awareness."

This brings me to the final brain-wave pattern to introduce, the pattern I call **the evolved mind**. This pattern is also a combination of beta, alpha, theta, and delta on the Mind Mirror. The difference between it and the awakened mind is that even more of the frequencies of each category are activated in a very organized, stabilized, and consistent way. By presenting a perfectly unified, symmetrical field of brain-wave frequencies, it provides a tangible demonstration through the brain-wave pattern itself of non-dualistic union. In other words, the unconscious has become conscious, and there is no division between the unconscious, the subconscious, and the conscious minds. The experience of this state is consistent with traditional descriptions of higher states of **samadhi** and **nirvana**.

This is not a state that even masters maintain while actively involved in their everyday affairs. This is not a pattern I look for, try to train, or even see very often. However, I have occasionally had a student in my class produce it and become overwhelmed by bliss. While monitoring Christian minister Rob Crickett's brain-wave patterns, I saw a graphic illustration of the progression from the awakened mind brain-wave pattern to the evolved mind brain-wave pattern. It was a beautiful and subtle transformation to watch on the Mind Mirror. When I asked him what he had experienced, he said that he "became one with the Paradise Father" and that this feeling was "beyond enlightenment."

World-renowned futurist, social innovator, and cofounder of The Foundation for Conscious Evolution, Barbara Marx Hubbard often spent time in this evolved brain-wave pattern while we worked together. In a poetic meditation from her book *Awakening Our Social Potential,* she writes, "I am a universal human. I am a new being upon this Earth. I have come forth from the whole process of creation. I am fifteen billion years old." This is certainly about finding the face you had before you were born.

Occasionally, masters go into this blissful, evolved mind brain-wave pattern while simply meditating. Professor Chen, the physics professor I mentioned in the Introduction who I did not realize was a Chi Kung master, produced a perfect evolved mind brain-wave pattern within one minute of closing his eyes.

ACCELERATING AWAKENING

My students occasionally joke at the end of a five-day seminar, "Well, that cuts out ten years of sitting in the cave!" But that joke is not so far from the truth. When you integrate the two aspects of consciousness—state and content—and use them together to help each other, you can move much farther much faster in the direction of your awakening.

You do not have to sit and wait for awakening to happen to you. Nor does it necessarily have to be elicited by a duplicitous dichotomy (as in the koan). "Source" or "spirit" can be sought, or more accurately, can be allowed in to your awareness. I work with the assumption that universal knowledge or divine access is not only consistently available to us if we know where to look and how to access it, but would also like us to find it. In other words, it's right there for the taking. We just have to unblock the blocks and get out of our own way.

It is also important to say that I still believe some element of grace is involved in your journey to awakening—that you cannot do it all in a predetermined scientific fashion. There are many more factors at play besides the state and content of consciousness—heart, spirit, and divine source to name a few. However, if we can scientifically speed up the development of the proper state by many years *and* we can work with content consciously, intentionally, and effectively, rather than just waiting for an act of grace, we have truly taken awakening the mind into the twenty-first century.

THE EXPANSION AND CONTRACTION OF CONSCIOUSNESS

The principle behind this meditation is to allow you to expand your energy in order to connect with your higher self/godhead/spiritual source and then contract again into your finite incarnate being to bring that spirituality and infinite wisdom into the corporeal details of everyday life.

Relax deeply.
Use your landmarks to help guide you down quickly and
    effortlessly into a deeply relaxed meditative state.
Allow yourself to let go of all spiritual goals and personal
    expectations.
Just become present inside yourself, right here, right now.

From here, begin to allow yourself to expand.
You may feel the expansion first in your body—
It's almost a sense of growing . . . larger and larger . . .
You may feel the expansion in your energy system—
Moving upward and outward as if to follow a column of light up
    through your spine and out the top of your head.

You may feel it as an expansion of a bubble around you,
in all directions at once.

You may experience it almost as a sense of "going home" . . .
A return to the light.

You may now begin to experience it as a sense of reaching upward
    and outward to your higher self . . .
And as you reach out to your higher self, you realize that your
    higher self is at the same time reaching down to you.
Your higher self wishing to make connection with you just as you
    wish to make connection with it . . .

Experiencing the union that is your birthright . . .
your origin . . .
your home . . .

And now from this expanded perspective, you can begin to get in
  touch with the infinite . . .

The universal . . .

You can feel the flow of rightness . . .
The sense of being on the correct path . . .
Or in the right Tao . . .

You can begin to have a sense of the big picture . . .
. . . a kind of knowledge of the cosmos . . .

Leading you to a sense of source . . .
A sense of the Godhead . . .

No matter what name or names you choose to use . . .
Peace . . .
Love . . .
God . . .
Divinity . . .
Higher Power . . .
Source . . .
Essence . . .

  . . . one of the thousand names of god . . .

You can begin to experience universal wisdom . . .

Just allow yourself now to spend a few minutes in this state of
  harmony and bliss . . .

■   ■   ■

Here, from this perspective, everything is right . . .
In perfect order . . .

You may see with absolute clarity of vision,
Or it may be blurred in blissful equanimity,

But your understanding is complete
A sense of satisfaction and peacefulness prevails.

■   ■   ■

And now, you begin to gaze down upon the smaller, more
    contracted world of your incarnate self.

And it gently and slowly begins to become clear how right things
    are down there, too.

You feel at once magnificently, endlessly, boundlessly large . . .
And yet intimate and comfortable in the humanness of your
    incarnate being . . .
    . . . at home.

■   ■   ■

You can, if you wish, now look down and begin to see your smaller
    self struggling with something . . .
some confusion or difficulty or tension that would have normally
    caused a problem.

You can, if you wish, drop a line of connection, like a plum line or a
    ray of awareness,

down to him or her, filling your smaller self with universal
consciousness

So that you have both at the same time . . .
Simultaneously aware of the expanded and the contracted,
The infinite and the finite,
The transcendent and the earthbound.

Awareness of both,
A union of both,

A merging of your higher self with that which is small in you,

An integration of your access to divinity with your earthly self.

■   ■   ■

And allow yourself now to have a new perspective . . .
A higher awareness . . .
A greater and more spiritual understanding . . .
of your incarnate issues
and corporeal experience.

You may now choose to bring this universal wisdom to any other
aspect of yourself that you wish . . .

And in this way, you may continue at any time to bring God
consciously into your everyday life.

REVIEW AND CLOSURE

A Reference Guide to Meditations

A *wakening the Mind* has been a "Guide to Mastering the Power of Your Brain Waves." From the Introduction, where you learned the theory and history behind this work, to the final chapters, where you experienced meditating on the qualities of mastery and the expansion and contraction of consciousness, this book has been teaching you to awaken your mind.

You may want to return again and again to this book, reviewing all or just specific parts as they apply to your needs at the time. These meditations are written so that they can be repeated many times and still be of fresh benefit each time you practice them. Whenever you meditate, allow yourself to experience every meditation as new, no matter how many times you have practiced it. Every time you practice a meditation, you are training the brain-wave state of consciousness that this particular meditation is designed to develop.

At this point, however, it might be valuable for you to review what you have gained from the meditations in the whole book. Doing so will help you integrate what you have learned and make it even more a part of you.

So, as you read through this review of the meditations, allow yourself to consider what you have experienced, what you learned, and what was most important for you in reading this book. Think about what you take away with you from this book, and how you can integrate that into your daily life.

As you reflect on all of the various aspects of this material, allow yourself to crystallize that which was most important for you. When you have finished reading the review, allow yourself to put into key words or images those things that you learned that were most important, most useful, and most meaningful to you in your everyday life. Consider how you can begin to integrate and apply this new learning.

REVIEW

Now allow yourself to remember way back to the beginning Introduction of this book. There you learned the theory of brain waves, the four categories of brain waves: beta, alpha, theta, and delta, and the combinations of brain waves for meditation and for the state of mastery called "the awakened mind."

In Chapter One, you learned about The Foundations of Mastery— Relaxing the Body and Stilling the Mind.

The meditations were:

> Deep Relaxation
>
> Becoming Aware of Thoughts
>
> Relaxing Your Tongue
>
> Counting Your Breath
>
> Slowing Your Breathing
>
> Withdrawal from Your Thoughts
>
> External Spot

Diffuse External Awareness

Internal Spot

Diffuse Internal Awareness

Internal and External

Mastering Beta with Imagery

In Chapter Two, you worked with Creating the Link to the Inner Self—Sensualization and the Development of Alpha Waves.

The meditations were:

Inside/Outside Visualization

Drink Sensualization

Sensualization Exercise

Spiritual Sensualization Exercise

Alpha Development Word Picture

Animal Sensualization

Alpha Eye Rolls

In Chapter Three, you learned about Accessing and Experiencing the Deep—Developing Theta Brain Waves.

The meditations were:

House of Doors

The Down and In Meditation

Healing Circle

Circle of Peace

Creativity Circle

In Chapter Four, we worked with developing Our Intuitive Radar—Exploring Delta Brain Waves.

The meditations were:

The Bubble

Gathering the Healing Energy for Transmission to Others

In Chapter Five, we learned about The Intricate Synthesis of Mastery—Beta, Alpha, Theta, and Delta, and the Awakened Mind.

The meditations were:

House of Doors II

Personal Transformation Meditation

Exercise Yo' Game

In Chapter Six, you worked with Self-Exploration and Understanding—Making the Subconscious Conscious.

The meditations were:

Animal Sensualization II

Plant/Tree Sensualization

Your Evolutionary Path

Finding the Block

In Chapter Seven, you worked with Healing the Blocks—Using Brain-Wave Development and Mastery for Personal Transformation and Change.

The meditations were:

> Transforming the Block
>
> Healing the Block
>
> Inner-Child Meditation

In Chapter Eight, you learned about Meditation and the Energy System—Awakening the Kundalini.

The meditations were:

> Meditation on the Chakras
>
> The Orbit
>
> Up and Out
>
> Kundalini Meditation

In Chapter Nine, we worked with Developing the Qualities of Mastery—The Fine Points of Awakening Your Mind.

The meditation was:

> The Qualities of Mastery

And in Chapter Ten, we explored Meditation and Awakening—A Bigger Picture.

The meditation was:

> The Expansion and Contraction of Consciousness

And here we are, finally, at the Review and Closure of *Awakening
the Mind*.

The meditation now is to consider what it is that you have learned
from reading this book,
what is important to you,
what you take away with you from this experience,
and how you can best integrate it into your everyday life.

Allow yourself to find a way to synthesize and crystallize
in a few words, images, or short sentences
that which was the most meaningful for your personal spiritual
evolution
and your development of mastery.

Be aware that in practicing these meditations,

you have been awakening your mind and mastering the power of
your brain waves . . .

Now, allow yourself to begin to consider where you choose to go
from here . . .

ANNA WISE has been teaching meditation and training brain waves for more than twenty-five years. She has a private practice and has led workshops, seminars, and corporate training worldwide. Anna began her search for an experience and understanding of the ineffable after a near-death experience at an early age. Her travels took her to England, where she began to work with the late C. Maxwell Cade and the Mind Mirror EEG in 1973. She moved to Boulder, Colorado, in 1981, where she was co-director of the Evolving Institute. By developing her understanding of the importance of the interrelationship between the state and the content of consciousness, Anna created her protocol for brain-wave training that forms the basis of her work. In 1988, she founded The Anna Wise Center, moving to San Francisco and finally settling in Marin County in 1990 with her son John. Over the next decade, Anna made her concepts concrete by writing *The High Performance Mind—Mastering Brainwaves for Insight, Healing, and Creativity;* designed her curriculum for training others to be practitioners; and traveled throughout the world, refining her understanding of mastery in order to complete *Awakening the Mind: A Guide to Mastering the Power of Your Brain Waves.*

CONTACT INFORMATION

The Anna Wise Center
1000A Magnolia Avenue
Larkspur, California 94939
Tel: (415)925-9449
Fax: (415)925-9355
www.annawise.com